Sigmund Freud

The Future of an Illusion

TRANSLATED BY J. A. UNDERWOOD
AND SHAUN WHITESIDE

PENGUIN BOOKS — GREAT IDEAS

PENGUIN BOOKS

Published by the Penguin Group
Penguin Books Ltd, 80 Strand, London WC2R ORL, England
Penguin Group (USA) Inc., 375 Hudson Street, New York, New York 10014, USA
Penguin Group (Canada), 90 Eglinton Avenue East, Suite 700, Toronto, Ontario, Canada M4P 2Y3
(a division of Pearson Penguin Canada Inc.)
Penguin Ireland, 25 St Stephen's Green, Dublin 2, Ireland
(a division of Penguin Books Ltd)
Penguin Group (Australia), 250 Camberwell Road, Camberwell, Victoria 3124, Australia
(a division of Pearson Australia Group Pty Ltd)
Penguin Books India Pvt Ltd, 11 Community Centre, Panchsheel Park, New Delhi – 110 017, India
Penguin Group (NZ), 67 Apollo Drive, Rosedale, North Shore 0632, New Zealand
(a division of Pearson New Zealand Ltd)
Penguin Books (South Africa) (Pty) Ltd, 24 Sturdee Avenue,
Rosebank, Johannesburg 2196, South Africa

Penguin Books Ltd, Registered Offices: 80 Strand, London WC2R ORL, England

www.penguin.com

'The Future of an Illusion' taken from *Mass Psychology and Other Writings*
This translation first published in Penguin Classics 2004
Translation © J. A. Underwood, 2004
'Mourning and Melancholia' taken from *On Murder, Mourning and Melancholia*
This translation first published in Penguin Classics 2005
Translation © Shaun Whiteside, 2005
Sigmund Freud's German texts collected in *Gesammelte Werke* (1940–52) © Imago
Publishing Co. Ltd, London, 1940, 1946, 1950
This edition first published 2008

010

All rights reserved

The moral right of the translators has been asserted

Set by Rowland Phototypesetting Ltd, Bury St Edmunds, Suffolk
Printed in England by Clays Ltd, St Ives plc

978-0-141-03676-2

www.greenpenguin.co.uk

MIX
Paper from
responsible sources
FSC
www.fsc.org
FSC® C018179

Penguin Books is committed to a sustainable
future for our business, our readers and our planet.
This book is made from Forest Stewardship
Council™ certified paper.

PENGUIN BOOKS — GREAT IDEAS

The Future of an Illusion

Sigmund Freud

1856–1939

Contents

The Future of an Illusion

I

Having lived for quite some time within a specific culture and tried repeatedly to study the nature of its origins and the path of its development, one also feels tempted just occasionally to turn and look in the other direction and ask what fate has in store for that culture and what changes it is destined to undergo. One quickly becomes aware, however, that any such venture is invalidated from the outset by several factors, chief among which is that only a few individuals are capable of commanding an overview of human activity in all its ramifications. Most people have found it necessary to concentrate on one or a small number of fields; yet the less a person knows about past and present, the shakier that person's judgement will inevitably be with regard to the future. Another factor is that, in this judgement in particular, the subjective expectations of the individual play a role that is hard to assess; yet those expectations turn out to depend on purely personal elements in an individual's own experience, his or her more or less hopeful attitude to life, as dictated by temperament and by degree of success or lack of it. Lastly, there is the effect of the remarkable fact that people in general experience their present almost naively, unable to appreciate what it holds; they must first put some distance between it and them – in other words, the present must first have become the past before it will furnish clues for assessing what is to come.

So anyone yielding to the temptation to pronounce on the probable future of our culture will do well to bear in mind the reservations outlined above – likewise the uncertainty that, as a general rule, attaches to any prediction. The consequence for me is that, in my haste to flee this excessive task, I shall swiftly resort to the smaller, more restricted area on which my attention has been focused hitherto, having first determined where that area lies in relation to the larger picture.

We know that human culture, by which I mean everything in which human life has risen above its animal circumstances and in which it distinguishes itself from animal life (and I refuse to separate culture and civilization), shows the observer two sides. It includes on the one hand all the knowledge and skill that humanity has acquired in order to control the forces of nature and obtain from it goods to satisfy human needs, and on the other hand all the institutions that are required to govern the relations of human beings one to another and in particular the distribution of such goods as can be obtained. The two directions of culture are not independent of each other, firstly because the mutual relations of human beings are extensively influenced by the amount of drive-satisfaction made possible by the commodities available, secondly because the individual human being can himself, vis-à-vis another person, assume the relationship of a commodity in so far as that other person makes use of the said individual's labour or takes the individual as sexual object, but thirdly because every individual is, in virtual terms, an enemy of culture, which is in fact supposed to constitute a universal human interest. It is a curious fact that human beings, incapable of living in individual isolation, nevertheless find the sacrifices that culture asks of them in order to make human co-existence possible a heavy load to bear. Culture, in other words, needs to be defended against the individual, and its arrangements, institutions and decrees all serve that end. Their purpose is not only to put in place a certain distribution of goods but also to maintain it; there is a need, in fact, for them to protect against the hostile impulses of humanity everything that serves to tame nature and generate commodities. Human creations are easily destroyed, and science and technology, having built them up, can also be used to tear them down.

This gives the impression that culture is something imposed on a reluctant majority by a minority that has managed to gain possession of the instruments of power and coercion. The natural assumption is of course that these difficulties are not of the essence of culture itself but spring from the imperfections of the forms of culture developed hitherto. Indeed, it is not hard to demonstrate such shortcomings. Whereas humanity has made continuous advances in controlling nature and can expect to make even greater ones, similar progress in the government of human affairs cannot be ascertained with any certainty, and it has doubtless always been the case (as it is again today) that many people wonder whether this bit of their cultural inheritance is in fact worth defending.

One would think that some rearrangement of human relationships must be possible such as would cause the sources of dissatisfaction with culture to dry up by renouncing coercion and the suppression of drives and allowing people to devote themselves to acquiring and enjoying commodities undisturbed by inner discord. That would be the Golden Age, except that one wonders whether such a condition can ever be realized. It seems instead that every culture must be based on coercion and drive renunciation; it does not even appear certain that, with coercion removed, the majority of human beings will be prepared to take upon themselves the labour that must be performed if greater quantities of essential commodities are to be obtained. We need in my view to accept that destructive (i.e. anti-social and anti-cultural) tendencies are present in all human beings and that in a large proportion of people such tendencies are powerful enough to dictate their behaviour within human society.

This psychological fact assumes crucial importance as regards assessing human culture. Whereas our first impression was that the key thing about culture was the conquest of nature in order to obtain the commodities essential to life and that the dangers threatening culture could be removed by effective distribution of such goods among human beings, the emphasis now seems to have shifted away from the material towards the mental. It becomes crucial whether and to what extent the burden of the libidinal sacrifices imposed on human beings can be successfully lightened and human beings reconciled to and compensated for the part of that burden that inevitably remains. Domination of the mass by a minority can no more be dispensed with than coercion to perform cultural work, because masses are lethargic and unreasonable, they are averse to renouncing their drives, they cannot be persuaded by arguments that this is unavoidable, and individuals within masses reinforce one another in giving free rein to their lack of restraint. Only the influence of exemplary individuals whom they accept as their leaders will induce them to perform the labour and suffer the voluntary privations on which the continued existence of culture depends. It is all very well, such leaders being persons with a superior understanding of the necessities of life who have brought themselves under control so far as their own libidinal desires are concerned. However, there is a risk so far as they are concerned that, in order to retain their influence, they will yield to the mass more than the mass yields to them, which is why it seems necessary for them to have access to instruments of power making them independent of the mass. In short, two very common properties of human beings are to blame for the fact that only through a measure of coercion can cultural institutions be upheld: humans are not, of their own volition, keen on work, and arguments are powerless against their passions.

I know what will be said against these remarks. The objection will be raised that the character of human masses as portrayed here, which supposedly proves the indispensability of coercion for cultural activity, is itself simply the result of defective cultural institutions that have made human beings bitter, vindictive and unapproachable. Fresh generations, full of love and brought up to respect intellectual achievement, having early experience of the benefits of culture, will also have a different attitude towards it; they will see it as their very own possession, and they will be prepared to offer it the sacrifices of labour and libidinal satisfaction required for its preservation. They will be able to dispense with coercion and will differ little from their leaders. If human masses of such quality have not existed in any culture hitherto, the reason is that no culture has yet hit upon the institutions that will influence people in such a way – and do so from childhood on.

One may doubt whether it is at all or indeed already (given the present state of our control over nature) possible to produce such cultural institutions, one may wonder where they are to come from, this body of superior, rock-steady, selfless leaders who will need to educate future generations, one may shrink from the appalling amount of coercion that will become unavoidable if such plans are ever to be implemented. The splendour of the intention and its importance for the future of human culture are beyond dispute. It rests securely on the psychological insight that humans are equipped with the most diverse libidinal predispositions, which the experiences of early childhood point in their final direction. The limits of human educability will therefore also define the effectiveness of any such cultural change. It may be doubted whether and to what extent a different cultural environment will be capable of erasing the two qualities of human masses that make leadership of human affairs so difficult. The experiment has never been made. In all probability, a certain percentage of human beings will always (because of morbid predispositions or excessively powerful drives) remain asocial, but even if we simply manage to bring today's anti-cultural majority down to a minority we shall have achieved a great deal – possibly all that can be achieved.

I do not want to give the impression that I have wandered a long way from the path of my investigation, as announced above. So let me say expressly that I have no intention of passing judgement on the great cultural experiment currently being conducted in the stretch of land between Europe and Asia. I have neither the knowledge nor the ability to pronounce on its feasibility, to examine the suitability of the methods being applied, or to measure the inevitable gulf between plan and execution. What is happening there, being incomplete, does not allow of the kind of consideration for which our long-consolidated culture presents the material.

II

Suddenly, we have slipped out of the economic sphere and into the psychological. We were tempted at first to look for the content of culture in terms of the commodities available and the institutions set up to distribute them. With the recognition that every culture rests on an obligation to work and on a renunciation of drives and therefore inevitably evokes opposition in the person to whom those demands apply, it became clear that commodities themselves, the means of obtaining them, and the arrangements for their distribution cannot be the essential or sole constituent of culture. The reason is that they are under threat from the rebelliousness and addiction to destruction of culture's co-owners. In addition to commodities we now have the means that can serve to defend the culture, the instruments of coercion and other instruments charged with the task of reconciling people to it and compensating them for their sacrifices. The latter, however, may be described as the mental property of culture.

In the interests of a uniform mode of expression, let us call the fact that a drive cannot be satisfied 'denial', the institution that lays down that denial a 'ban', and the state that the ban brings about 'privation'. The next

step is then to distinguish between privations that affect
everyone and privations that do not affect everyone but
only groups, classes, or even individuals. The former are
the oldest: with the bans that they imposed, culture
began the process of separation from the brutish primal
state, no one knows how many thousands of years ago.
To our surprise, we found that they are still influential,
still form the nucleus of hostility to culture. The libidinal
desires that suffer thereunder are reborn with every
child; there is a class of people, namely neurotics, who
react even to these denials with anti-social behaviour.
Such libidinal desires are those of incest, cannibalism and
bloodlust. It sounds strange that these desires, condemn-
nation of which appears to attract universal agreement,
should be bracketed together with others, the granting
or denial of which is so vehemently fought over in our
culture, yet in psychological terms this is justified. Nor
is the cultural stance adopted towards these earliest
libidinal desires by any means uniform: only cannibalism
seems universally frowned on and beyond all non-
analytical examination, while the strength of incestuous
desires may still be sensed behind the ban, and murder
is under certain circumstances still practised (indeed,
preached) in our culture. The future may well hold
in store for us cultural developments in which other,
currently quite possible satisfactions of desire will seem
as unacceptable as that of cannibalism does today.

Even in connection with these oldest drive-
renunciations, a psychological factor comes into consideration that retains its significance for all the rest as
well. It is not true that the human mind had undergone

no development since the earliest times and in contrast to the advances made by science and technology is the same today as at the beginning of history. One such mental advance can be demonstrated here. It lies in the direction of our evolution that external coercion is gradually internalized in that a specific mental agency, namely the human Above-'I', takes it under its command. Every child acts out for us the process of such a change; in fact, it is what makes the child a moral and social being. This strengthening of the Above-'I' is an extremely valuable psychological piece of cultural content. The persons in whom it has occurred turn from being enemies of culture to being upholders of culture. The more numerous they are in a given cultural environment, the more secure that culture will be and the more likely it is to be able to dispense with external instruments of coercion. Now, the degree of such internalization varies widely so far as individual libidinal bans are concerned. As regards the oldest cultural requirements mentioned above, internalization (leaving aside the unwelcome exception of neurotics) seems largely complete. The situation changes when one turns to the other libidinal demands. One then notices with surprise and concern that a majority of people will heed the relevant cultural bans only under pressure from external coercion – in other words, only where such pressure is able to make itself felt and so long as it inspires fear. The same applies with regard to those so-called 'moral' cultural requirements that are set for everyone similarly. Most of what is said about the moral unreliability of human beings belongs here. Untold numbers of civilized human beings who would recoil from murder or incest do not deny themselves satisfaction of their greed, aggression or sexual desires and will not hesitate to harm others through lying, cheating and calumny, if they can get away with it, and this has doubtless always been the case, through many cultural epochs.

As regards restrictions that relate only to specific classes of society, the circumstances encountered are obvious as well as being never missed. It is to be expected that these neglected classes will envy the privileged their prerogatives and do everything to be rid of their own greater degree of privation. Where this is not possible, a permanent measure of dissatisfaction will assert itself within that culture that may lead to dangerous rebellions. However, if a culture has not got beyond the point where the satisfaction of some participants requires the oppression of others, maybe the majority (and this is the case with all contemporary cultures), then, understandably, the oppressed will develop a deep hostility towards a culture that their labour makes possible but in whose commodities they have too small a share. In that case, no internalization of cultural bans can be expected among the oppressed; indeed, they will be loath to acknowledge those bans, striving instead to destroy the culture itself, and in the end abolishing its very premises. The anti-cultural stance of such classes is so evident that what tends to be the latent hostility of the better-served strata of society has been overlooked on that account. It goes without saying that a culture that fails to satisfy so many participants, driving them to rebellion, has no chance of lasting for any length of time, nor does it deserve one.

The degree of internalization of cultural precepts (to use a popular, non-psychological phrase: the moral level of participants) is not the only mental asset to be taken into consideration when it comes to appraising a culture. There is also its wealth of ideals and artistic creations – that is to say, the satisfactions derived from both.

People are over-inclined to place the ideals of a culture (i.e. its judgements as to which are the supreme achievements, those most worth striving for) among its psychological assets. It seems at first as if such ideals determine the achievements of the culture group; what actually happens, though, is probably that the ideals emerge in line with the earliest achievements made possible by the combined effects of a culture's inner aptitude and external circumstances, and that those earliest achievements are then captured by the ideal for continuation. In other words, the satisfaction that the ideal gives to those involved in a culture is narcissistic in nature, being based on pride in what has already been achieved. For it to be complete, it requires comparison with other cultures that have plumped for different achievements and evolved different ideals. On the strength of those differences, every culture gives itself the right to look down on the others. This is how cultural ideals occasion rupture and hostility between different culture groups – most obviously amongst nations.

Narcissistic satisfaction arising out of the cultural ideal is also one of the forces successfully countering cultural hostility within the culture group. Not only do the privileged classes, who enjoy the benefits of that culture, share in it; the oppressed may share in it, too, in that the right to despise outsiders is their compensation for the restrictions placed on them in their own circle. A person may be a poor plebeian, burdened by debts and compulsory military service, yet that person is a Roman and as such involved in the task of ruling over other nations and writing their laws. However, this identification of the oppressed with the class that controls and exploits them is only part of a larger context. On the other hand, the former may be emotionally bound to the latter; their hostility notwithstanding, they may see their masters as embodying their ideals. Without such basically satisfactory relationships, it would be a mystery why certain cultures survived for so long, despite justified hostility on the part of large sections of the population.

Different again is the satisfaction that art gives those involved in a culture group, though as a rule this remains beyond the reach of the masses, who are preoccupied by exhausting labour and have received no personal education. Art, as we learned long ago, offers substitute satisfactions for the oldest, still most deeply felt cultural renunciations and therefore has a uniquely reconciling effect with the sacrifices made for it. On the other hand, its creations boost the identification feelings of which every culture group stands in such need by fostering impressions that are experienced jointly and held in high esteem; but they also contribute to narcissistic satisfaction if they represent the achievements of the particular culture, offering impressive reminders of its ideals.

Possibly the most important item in the psychical inventory of a culture has yet to be mentioned. This is what in the broadest sense constitutes its ideas about religion – in other words (words that will require justification at a later stage), that culture's illusions.

III

What constitutes the special value of religious ideas?

We have spoken of hostility to culture, engendered by the pressure that a culture exerts, the libidinal renunciations that it demands. Imagining its bans lifted, a man is free to choose any woman he wishes as sexual object; he may without compunction strike his rivals for the woman dead or kill anyone else who stands in his way, and he may help himself to any of his neighbour's goods without asking permission. How splendid, what a string of satisfactions life would then have to offer! Before long, of course, the next problem emerges. Everyone else has precisely the same desires as myself and will give me no more quarter than I give him. Basically, this means that only a single individual can derive unrestricted happiness from such a removal of cultural restrictions, a tyrant, a dictator who has grabbed all the instruments of power for himself, and even he has every reason to hope that others will respect at least one cultural ban: the one saying 'you shall not kill'.

But how ungrateful (how short-sighted, in fact) to strive for an abolition of culture! What is left then is the state of nature, and that is far harder to bear. Granted, nature would demand no drive-restrictions of us, it would leave us be, but nature has its own particularly effective way of placing restrictions on us: it kills us – coldly, cruelly, without a qualm, it seems to us – perhaps on the very occasions of our satisfaction. It was precisely because of the perils with which nature threatens us that we got together in the first place and created culture, which is meant among other things to enable us to live together. Indeed, the main function of culture, the real reason for its existence, is to shield us against nature.

As we know, it already does a pretty good job of that now in many respects and will one day, clearly, do a far better one. But no one succumbs to the deluded belief that nature has already been conquered; few dare hope that it will one day be wholly subject to the human race. There are the elements, which appear to mock any kind of human constraint: earth, which heaves and splits open, burying all things human and all the works of humankind; water, which when in tumult swamps and drowns everything; storms, which blow everything away; there are diseases, which we have only recently come to recognize as attacks by other living creatures, and finally there is the painful riddle of death, against which no remedy has yet been found, nor probably ever will. These powers nature lines up against us, magnificent, cruel, relentless, reminding us of our weakness and of the helplessness we had thought our cultural activities would overcome. One of the few pleasing and uplifting impressions furnished by the human race is when, faced with an elemental disaster, it forgets its cultural muddle-headedness and all its internal problems and enmities and recalls the great common task of preserving itself against the superior might of nature.

As for humanity as a whole, so too for the individual human, life is hard to bear. A certain amount of privation is imposed on him by the culture to which he belongs, some suffering is heaped on him by other people, either despite the rules laid down by that culture or because of that culture's imperfection. In addition, there is what untamed nature (he calls it fate) does him in the way of harm. A constant state of fearful expectation and some severe injury to natural narcissism should follow from such a condition. We already know how the individual reacts to the damage inflicted on him by culture and by other people: he develops a corresponding degree of resistance to the institutions of that culture, of hostility to culture. But how does he defend himself against the superior forces of nature, of fate, which threaten him like everyone else?

Culture does the job for him; it does it for everyone in the same way; in fact, remarkably, more or less all cultures are alike in this. For instance, culture does not cease to operate once it has performed its task of defending the individual human against nature; it simply continues that task by other means. In this case, the task is a multiple one: man's badly threatened self-esteem craves consolation, the world and life need to lose their terror, and at the same time humanity's thirst for knowledge, which is of course driven by the strongest practical interest, craves an answer.

With the first step, much is already gained. And that is to humanize nature. Impersonal forces and fates are unapproachable, they remain forever alien. But if passions rage in the elements as they do in the human heart, if even death is not something spontaneous but an act of violence perpetrated by an evil will, if everywhere in nature a person is surrounded by beings like those he knows from his own society, then he will breathe easier, feel at home in quite unfamiliar surroundings, be able, mentally, to deal with his irrational fears; a person may still be defenceless but he is not helpless any longer, not paralysed, he can at least react. In fact, he may not even be defenceless: he can deploy against those violent supermen out there the same resources as he uses in his society. He can try beseeching them, appeasing them, bribing them; by exerting such influence, he will rob them of some of their power. That kind of replacement of a natural science by psychology not only brings immediate relief; it also points the way towards further coping with the situation.

Because there is nothing new about this situation, it has its model in infancy, it is simply a continuation of an earlier situation, in fact; one had experienced this kind of helplessness back then, as a small child facing parents whom one had reason to fear (particularly the male parent), but of whose protection one was also confident in the face of the dangers one was aware of at the time. So the obvious thing was to compare the two situations. Also, as in dream life, wish then got its money's worth, so to speak. A premonition of death assails the sleeper, wanting to put him in the grave, but dream work is able to select the condition in which even this feared event becomes wish-fulfilment; the dreamer sees himself in an ancient Etruscan tomb into which, happy to have his archaeological interests catered to, he had descended. Similarly, a person does not simply turn the forces of nature into people among whom he is able to move as amongst his peers; that would not do justice, in fact, to the overpowering impression he has of them. Instead, he invests them with a paternal character, turning them into gods, and in the process following not only an infantile model but also, as I have tried to show, a phylogenetic model.

In time, the first observations of regularity in natural phenomena are made; they are found to conform to laws, and the forces of nature lose their human traits as a result. However, the helplessness felt by human beings remains, as do their paternal yearnings and the gods. The latter retain their triple function of warding off the terrors of nature, reconciling humans to the cruelty of fate, notably as revealed in death, and compensating them for the sufferings and privations imposed upon them by living together in a culture group.

Little by little, though, the emphasis within the exercise of those functions shifts. People notice that natural phenomena develop spontaneously in accordance with inner necessities; the gods are still the lords of nature, they set nature up in a certain way and they can now leave it to itself. Only occasionally do they intervene in its course, working what are called miracles, as if to affirm that they have surrendered none of their original power. As regards the distribution of fates, there remains an uncomfortable suspicion that the bewilderment and helplessness of the human race is beyond remedy. This is where the gods fail most; if they themselves create fate, it has to be said that their ways are mysterious; the most gifted nation in the ancient world glimpsed dimly that *Moira* stands above the gods and that the gods themselves have their fates. And the more nature becomes autonomous, with the gods withdrawing from it, the more earnestly all expectations focus on the third function attributed to them and the more the moral sphere becomes their proper domain. The task of the gods now becomes to make good the ills and shortcomings of culture, to heed the sufferings that people inflict on one another in living together, and to supervise implementation of the rules of culture with which humans find it so hard to comply. The rules of culture are themselves deemed to be of divine provenance; exalted above human society, they are extended to nature and world events.

In this way a treasury of ideas is created, born of the need to make human helplessness bearable, its building materials memories of everyone's own helplessness and that of the childhood of the human race. Quite obviously, this possession shields man in two directions: against the perils of nature and fate and against the damage inflicted by human society itself. In context, the message is: life in this world serves a higher purpose, one not easy to guess, admittedly, but without doubt implying a perfection of human nature. Probably the spiritual side of humanity, the soul, which has slowly and reluctantly separated from the body down the ages, is the intended object of such elevation and enhancement. Everything that happens in this world does so in execution of the intentions of a higher intelligence that, albeit in ways (including some roundabout ways) that are hard to follow, ultimately steers it all in the direction of the good, i.e. that which is gratifying to ourselves. A benevolent and only apparently strict Providence watches over us all, not permitting us to become the plaything of all-powerful, pitiless natural forces; death itself is no destruction, no return to inorganic lifelessness, but the start of a new kind of existence situated on the path to higher development. Conversely, the same moral laws as our cultures have drawn up also govern all that happens in the world, the only difference being that a supreme judicial instance watches over them with incomparably greater might and rigour. In the end, everything good will find its reward, everything evil its punishment, if not in this form of life then in later existences that start after death. This means that all life's terrors, sufferings and hardships are destined to be obliterated; life after death, which extends our earthly existence just as the invisible part of the spectrum is appended to the visible, will bring all the perfection that we may have missed here. And the superior wisdom that guides this process, the universal goodness that finds expression in it, the justice that finds implementation through it – these are the properties of the divine beings that also created ourselves and the world as a whole. Or rather, of the one divine being into which in our culture all the gods of earlier times have become compressed. The people that first achieved this concentration of divine properties was not a little proud of such progress. It had exposed the paternal core that had always lain hidden behind every god figure; basically, this was a return to the historical beginnings of the god idea. With God now a single being, relations towards him could recover the intimacy and intensity of the child's relationship with its father. But having done so much for their father, folk wanted to be rewarded, they wanted at least to become the only beloved child, the chosen people. Many centuries later, a pious America claimed to be 'God's own country', and for one of the forms in which humans worship the deity that is indeed true.

The religious ideas summarized above naturally went through a lengthy development, and different cultures captured them in different phases. I have extracted a single such phase of development, corresponding approximately to the end result in our present-day white Christian culture. It is easy to see that not all pieces of that entity fit equally well together, that not all pressing questions are answered, that the inconsistency of everyday experience can be dismissed only with difficulty. But such as they are these ideas (religious in the broadest sense) are reckoned the most precious possession of culture, the most valuable thing it has to offer its participants, held in far higher esteem than all the skills of parting the earth from its treasures, feeding humanity, fending off disease, etc. People think life is unbearable unless they attach to such ideas the value that is claimed for them. The question is: what are these ideas in the light of psychology, why are they held in such high esteem, and (venturing shyly on) what are they actually worth?

IV

An investigation that proceeds smoothly in the style of a monologue is not wholly risk-free. One is too tempted to brush aside ideas that would interrupt it, and in return one gets a feeling of uncertainty that one seeks in the end to drown out by being overly decisive. So I shall imagine an opponent who follows my remarks mistrustfully, and from time to time I shall give him the floor.

I hear him say: '*You have repeatedly used the expressions: culture creates these religious ideas, culture makes them available to its participants, there's something disconcerting about that; I couldn't say why myself, it doesn't sound as self-evident as that culture has made arrangements regarding the distribution of the product of labour or regarding rights to woman and child.*'

My view, however, is that one is entitled to use such expressions. I was trying to show that religious ideas sprang from the same necessity as all the other attainments of culture, from the need to mount a defence against the oppressive dominance of nature. There was a second motive, too, namely the urge to correct the painfully felt imperfections of culture. It is also particularly apt to say that culture bestows such ideas upon the individual, because the individual discovers them, they are brought to him complete, he would be incapable of finding them on his own. It is the legacy of many generations he is entering upon, taking it over like his multiplication tables, like geometry, etc. There is a difference here, of course, but it lies elsewhere and cannot yet be examined. You mention the sense of being disconcerted: that may have something to do with the fact that this body of religious ideas is usually presented to us as divine revelation. However, that is itself part of the religious system, it completely ignores what we know to have been the historical emergence of those ideas and the way they differed in different eras and cultures.

'Another point – more important, it seems to me. You make the humanization of nature proceed from the need to put an end to human bewilderment and helplessness in the face of its dreaded forces, establish a relationship with it, and eventually gain some influence over it. But that kind of motive seems superfluous. Primitive man, after all, has no choice, no other way of thinking. It is natural for him (innate, so to speak) to project his being out into the world and to regard every process that he observes as springing from beings basically similar to himself. That is the only way he can understand things. And it is by no means self-explanatory, in fact it is a remarkable coincidence, if by thus giving free rein to his natural disposition he should succeed in meeting one of his major needs.'

I do not find that so extraordinary. Do you believe, then, that a person's thinking has no practical motives, that it simply expresses a selfless curiosity? Surely that is highly unlikely? I take the view that, even when personifying the forces of nature, the human being is conforming to an infant model. Having learned from the people who made up his earliest environment that, if he established a relationship with them, that was the way to influence them, he subsequently, with the same intention, treated everything else he encounted in the same way as he had treated them. So I do not disagree with your descriptive comment, it really is natural to man to personify everything he seeks to understand with a view to controlling it afterwards (mental coping as preparation for physical), but I also provide the motive and genesis of that peculiarity of human thinking.

'And now a third thing. You dealt with the origins of religion before, in your book Totem and Taboo. But there the picture is different. Everything is the father-son relationship, God is the exalted father, yearning for a father is the root of religious need. Since then, apparently, you have discovered the element of human powerlessness and helplessness, to which the biggest role in the formation of religion is in fact generally ascribed, and now you shift on to helplessness everything that was once the father complex. Could you please tell me about this change?'

Willingly, I was just waiting for the challenge. If it really is a change. Totem and Taboo was meant to throw light not on the emergence of religions but only on that of totemism. Can you explain, from any of the standpoints known to you, why the first form in which protective divinity revealed itself to man was animal, why there was a ban on killing and eating that animal, and why it was nevertheless the solemn custom, once a year, to come together to kill and eat it? That is exactly what happens in totemism. And there is little point in arguing about whether totemism should be described as a religion. It is intimately related to the later divine religions, with the totem animals becoming the sacred animals of the gods. And the earliest but most deep-rooted moral restrictions (the bans on murder and incest) spring from the soil of totemism. Now, whether or not you accept the conclusions of *Totem and Taboo*, I hope you will concede that, in the book, a number of very remarkable scattered facts are brought together into a consistent whole.

Why the animal god was inadequate in the long run and was replaced by the human form is scarcely touched on in *Totem and Taboo*, while other problems of how religion took shape are not mentioned at all. In your eyes, is such a restriction tantamount to a denial? My work is a good example of strict isolation of the part that psychoanalytical examination can play in solving the problem of religion. If I now attempt to add the other, less deeply concealed part, you ought not to accuse me of contradiction – any more than of one-sidedness previously. It is my job (of course it is) to demonstrate the links between what I said earlier and what I am submitting now, between the underlying and the manifest motivation, between the father complex and human helplessness and need for protection.

Those links are not difficult to find. They are the connections between the helplessness of the child and that (perpetuating it) of the adult, with the result that, as was to be expected, the psychoanalytical motivation behind the formation of religion becomes the infantile contribution to its manifest motivation. Let us place ourselves in the inner life of the small child. You remember the choice of object in accordance with the support-seeking type that analysis talks about? The libido, following the paths of the narcissistic needs, attaches itself to the objects that promise to satisfy those needs. For example, the child's mother, who stills its hunger, becomes its first love-object and undoubtedly also its first protection against all the vague dangers that threaten it from the outside world – the child's first fear shield, we might say.

The mother is soon supplanted in this function by the stronger father, with whom it then remains right throughout childhood. However, the child's relationship to its father is burdened with a curious ambivalence. The father was himself a danger, possibly because of the earlier relationship to the mother. As a result, the child fears him no less than it yearns for and admires him. The signs of this ambivalence in the father relationship are deeply embedded in all religions, as is also explained in *Totem and Taboo*. If as a person grows older he realizes that he is destined to remain a child for ever, that he can never manage without protection against alien superior powers, he invests those powers with the traits of the father-figure, creating for himself gods of whom he is afraid, whom he seeks to win over, and to whom he nevertheless assigns his protection. The motif of yearning for the father is thus identical with the need for protection against the consequences of human power-lessness; the defence provided against infant helplessness gives the reaction to the helplessness that the young adult is forced to acknowledge (i.e. the formation of religion) its characteristic features. However, it is not our intention to explore the development of the God notion any further; what concerns us here is the complete treasury of religious ideas as transmitted to the individual by his culture.

V

To resume the thread of our investigation – what, then, is the psychological significance of religious ideas, how are we to classify them? The question is by no means easy to answer at first. After rejecting various formulations, we are left with one only: they are dogmas, statements about facts and circumstances of external (or internal) reality that convey something we have not discovered for ourselves and that demand to be believed. Since they impart information about what is most important and most interesting for us in life, they are valued particularly highly. Whoever knows nothing of them is deeply ignorant; whoever has taken them on board as knowledge may consider himself greatly enriched.

Of course, there are many such dogmas regarding a wide variety of things in this world. Every school lesson is full of them. Take geography, for instance. There we are told: Constance lies on the Bodensee. As the German student song says: 'If you don't believe it, go and see!' I do happen to have been there and can confirm that that beautiful city does indeed lie on the shore of a broad stretch of water that all who live around it call 'the Bodensee'. I too am now wholly convinced of the correctness of that geographical assertion. I am reminded of another, very remarkable experience in this connection. It was as a grown-up man that I first stood on the hill of the Athenian Acropolis, surrounded by ruined temples, gazing out over the blue sea. Mingled with my happiness was a sense of astonishment that came to me as: so it really is true, what we were taught at school! How shallow, how feeble must have been the belief I had acquired then in the actual truth of what I was being told for me to feel such surprise now! Yet I am reluctant to over-stress the significance of that experience; a different explanation for my astonishment is possible – one that did not occur to me at the time, is thoroughly subjective in character, and has to do with the exceptional nature of the place.

Thus all such dogmas demand belief in their content, though not without justifying their claim. They present themselves as the abbreviated outcome of a longer thought process based on observation as well as, no doubt, on inference; if a person means to go through the process for himself rather than accept the result, they show that person how. And invariably one is also told where the knowledge that the dogma proclaims comes from, unless, as with geographical assertions, that goes without saying. For example, the earth is in the shape of a ball; proofs advanced are Foucault's pendulum, the behaviour of the horizon, and the possibility of sailing around the world. Since all concerned agree that it is not feasible to send all schoolchildren off on voyages of circumnavigation, it is felt sufficient to have the teaching of the classroom accepted 'in good faith' – but in the knowledge that the path to personal conviction remains open.

Let us try gauging the dogmas of religion by the same measure. When we ask what their claim to be believed is based on, we receive three answers that are oddly out of harmony with one another. Firstly, they are worthy of belief because our forefathers believed in them back then; secondly, we possess proof handed down to us from that same dim and distant time; and thirdly, it is forbidden to ask for such authentication anyway. This kind of undertaking was once punished with the utmost severity, and even today society frowns on anyone trying it again.

This third point inevitably arouses our strongest misgivings. There can only ever be one motive for such a ban, namely that society is well aware of the shakiness of the claim it makes for its religious teachings. Otherwise it would surely have no hesitation in providing anyone who wished to form his own conviction with the necessary means. So it is with a mistrust that will not be easy to assuage that we set about examining the other two arguments. We are asked to believe because our forefathers believed. Yet those ancestors of ours were far less knowledgeable than ourselves, they believed in things that we, today, cannot anyhow accept. It is at least possible that religious teachings, too, might be of such a kind. The proofs they bequeath to us are enshrined in writings that themselves bear all the signs of unreliability. They are full of contradictions and have been reworked and adulterated; where they speak of actual attestations they are themselves unattested. It is not much help if, for their wording or even simply for their content, the provenance of divine revelation is asserted, since that assertion itself forms part of the teachings that are to be examined as to their credibility – and no proposition, as we know, can prove itself.

This leads us to the odd conclusion that precisely those pronouncements from our cultural inheritance that might be of the greatest significance so far as we are concerned, communications whose allotted function is to explain to us the mysteries of the world and reconcile us to the tribulations of existence – precisely they have the feeblest authentication of all. We could never agree to accept a fact of such indifference to us as that whales give birth to young rather than lay eggs, were there no better proof of it than that.

This state of affairs constitutes a very remarkable psychological problem in itself. Nor should anyone think that the foregoing remarks about the unverifiable nature of religious teachings contain anything new. People have always been aware that they defy proof – as were, surely, the forefathers who bequeathed such an inheritance. Probably many of them harboured the same scepticism as we have ourselves, but the pressure on them was too great for them to dare voice their misgivings. And countless men and women have tormented themselves with identical doubts ever since, trying to suppress them because they felt under an obligation to believe; many brilliant intellects have met with defeat in this conflict, many individuals have been damaged by the compromises in which they sought a way out.

If all the proofs that are advanced for the credibility of religious doctrines stem from the past, the obvious course is to examine whether the present, which can be better assessed, is also capable of furnishing such proofs.

If one single component of the religious system could successfully be removed from doubt in this way, the whole would gain exceptionally in credibility. This is where the activities of spiritualists come in; convinced that the individual soul lives on, they seek to put this one proposition of religious teaching beyond doubt so far as we are concerned. Sadly, they cannot disprove that, when their spirits appear and say things, these are simply products of their own mental activity. They have cited the spirits of the greatest men, the most outstanding thinkers, but all the pronouncements and messages received from them have been so silly, so wretchedly uninformative, that we can find nothing that merits belief beyond the ability of such spirits to adapt themselves to the group invoking them.

At this point we must look at two tests that give the impression of making strenuous efforts to avoid the problem. One of these, violent in nature, is ancient, the other subtle and modern. The first is the Church Father's *credo quia absurdum*. This is supposed to mean that religious teachings escape the requirements of reason, they are above reason. Their truth must be felt inwardly, it need not be understood. However, this *credo* is interesting only as confession, as claim to power it is without obligation. Am I to be obliged to believe every absurdity? And if not, why this one in particular? There is no authority higher than reason. If the truth of religious teachings depends upon an inward experience attesting that truth, what about the many people who do not have so rare an experience? Everyone can be required to use the gift of reason that they possess, but an obligation that applies to all cannot be based on a motive that exists only for very few. If an individual has drawn from a deeply personal state of ecstasy the unshakeable conviction that the teachings of religion represent the real truth, what is that to the next man?

The second test is the 'as if' philosophy. This says that there are plenty of assumptions in our intellectual activity that we quite agree are unfounded, even absurd. They are called fictions, but for a variety of reasons we allegedly have to act 'as if' we believed those fictions. This (we are told) applies with regard to the teachings of religion because of their incomparable importance as regards sustaining human society. This line of argument is not far removed from the *credo quia absurdum*. However, in my opinion the 'as if' demand is one that only a philosopher can make. Anyone whose thinking is not influenced by the arts of philosophy will never be able to accept it; so far as he is concerned the admission of absurdity, of being contrary to reason, is the end of the matter. Such a person cannot, particularly as regards treating his most important interests, be made to sacrifice the certainties that he otherwise requires for all his everyday activities. I remember how one of my children distinguished himself at an early age by attaching particular importance to objectivity. When the children were being told a story, to which they were listening with rapt attention, he would come up and ask: 'Is that a true story?' When this was denied, he assumed a scornful expression and withdrew. People can be expected before long to react to the 'story' of religion in a similar way, the 'as if' recommendation notwithstanding.

At present, however, they are still behaving quite otherwise, and back in past times religious ideas, for all their indisputable lack of attestation, exerted the most powerful influence on people. This is a new psychological problem. The question must be asked: wherein lies the inner strength of those teachings, to what do they owe an effectiveness that does not depend on acceptance by reason?

VI

We have made adequate preparations, I think, to answer both questions. The answer emerges if we examine the psychical genesis of religious ideas. Such ideas, which put themselves forward as dogmas, are not deposits from experience or end products of cogitation, they are illusions, fulfilling the oldest, most powerful, most pressing desires of the human race; the secret of their strength is the strength of those desires. We have seen already how the terrifying impression of helplessness in childhood awakened the need for protection (protection by love), which the father provided, and how awareness of the continuance of that helplessness throughout life prompted the adult to cling to the existence of another (this time mightier) father. Through the gracious action of divine providence fear of the perils of life is allayed, the appointment of a moral world order guarantees fulfilment of the demand for justice that has so often remained unfulfilled within human culture, while prolonging earthly existence by means of a future life provides the spatial and temporal framework within which such wish-fulfilment shall occur. Answers to riddles posed by man's thirst for knowledge, such as how the world came into being and the nature of the relationship between body and mind, are developed in accordance with the premises of this system; it represents a wonderful relief for the individual psyche when the never entirely surmounted conflicts of childhood arising out of the father complex are lifted from its shoulders, so to speak, and fed into a solution that is accepted by everyone.

If I say they are all illusions, I must define the meaning of the word. An illusion is not the same as an error, nor is it necessarily an error. Aristotle's view that filth engenders vermin (which the ignorant masses entertain to this day) was an error, as was that of an earlier medical generation that *Tabes dorsalis*[1] resulted from sexual excess. It would be incorrect to call such errors illusions. On the other hand, it was an illusion on Columbus's part that he had discovered a new sea route to India. How much what he wished for contributed to that error is very clear. It is possible to describe as an illusion the assertion made by certain nationalists that the Indo-Germanic race is the only one capable of culture, or the belief (which only psychoanalysis has demolished) that the child is a being without sexuality. Typically, the illusion is derived from human desires; in this respect it resembles the psychiatric delusion, though it also differs from it, quite apart from the more complicated structure of the latter. As the key feature of the delusion, we would stress its inconsistency with reality, while the illusion is not necessarily false, i.e. unrealizable or in conflict with reality. For example, a middle-class girl may entertain

[1] [A disease of the nervous system caused by advanced syphilis.]

the illusion that a prince will come to carry her off to his home. It is possible, cases of the sort have occurred. That the Messiah will come and establish a new golden age is far less likely; depending on the personal stance of the person assessing it, he will classify this belief as an illusion or as analogous to a delusion. Instances of illusions that have proved true are not normally easy to find. However, the alchemists' illusion (that they could turn all metals into gold) may be such a one. The desire to have a great deal of gold, as much gold as possible, has been much muted by our modern understanding of the conditions of wealth, yet chemistry no longer considers it impossible to turn metals into gold. In other words, we refer to a belief as an illusion when wish-fulfilment plays a prominent part in its motivation, and in the process we disregard its relationship to reality, just as the illusion itself dispenses with accreditations.

If, armed with this information, we return to the teachings of religion, we may say again: they are all illusions, unverifiable, no one should be forced to regard them as true, to believe in them. Some of them are so improbable, so contrary to everything that we have laboriously learned about the reality of the world, that (making due allowance for the psychological differences) they can be likened to delusions. The reality value of most of them cannot be assessed. Just as they are unverifiable, they are also irrefutable. Too little is known as yet to bring them into closer critical focus. The world's riddles unveil themselves only slowly to our researches, there are many questions science cannot yet answer. However, as we see it, scientific work is the sole avenue

that can lead to knowledge of the reality outside ourselves. Again, it is simply an illusion to expect anything
of intuition and immersion in the self; that can give us
nothing but (highly ambiguous) indications regarding
our own inner life, never information about the questions religious dogma finds it so easy to answer. To stick
one's own caprice in the gap and use private judgement
to pronounce this or that bit of the religious system
more or less acceptable would be a wanton undertaking.
Such questions are too significant for that – too holy,
one might almost say.

At this point, prepare for the objection: '*All right, if
even hardened sceptics admit that the claims of religion cannot
be refuted by reasoning, why should I not then believe those
claims on the grounds that they have so much in their favour:
tradition, popular agreement, and all the consolation that they
bring?*' Why not, indeed? Just as no one can be forced
into belief, nor can anyone be forced into disbelief.
However, let no one fall into the trap of assuming that
such arguments point the way to right thinking. If there
was ever a place for the 'feeble excuse' verdict, this is it.
Ignorance is ignorance; no right to believe something
can ever flow from it. No rational person will conduct
himself so frivolously in other matters and be content
with such miserable justifications of his judgements, his
partisanship; only in the highest and holiest matters does
anyone permit himself that. In reality, he is merely trying
to pretend to himself or others that he still holds fast to
religion, whereas he detached himself from it a while
back. When questions of religion are at issue, people
commit all kinds of insincerity, slip into all sorts of

intellectual bad habits. Philosophers stretch the mean-
ings of words until scarcely anything of the original sense
of those words is left; they call some vague abstraction
of their own invention 'God' and now they too are deists,
trumpeting their belief in God abroad, able to pride
themselves on having discerned a higher, purer concept
of God, despite the fact that their God is no more than
an insubstantial shadow, no longer the mighty figure of
religious teaching. Critics insist on describing as 'deeply
religious' a person who admits to a feeling of human
smallness and impotence in the face of the totality of the
world, although it is not that feeling that constitutes
religiousness but in fact the next step, the reaction to it:
seeking a remedy for the feeling. The person who does
not take that step but instead humbly accepts the minor
role of humanity in the wider world – that is the person
who is irreligious in the true sense of the word.

It forms no part of the intention of this study to
comment on the truth-value of religious teachings. We
are content to recognize that, psychologically speaking,
they are illusions. However, we need not conceal the
fact that this discovery will also greatly influence our
attitude towards the question that many must regard as
the one that matters most. We know approximately
when the teachings of religion were created and by what
kinds of people. If we go on to uncover the motives that
prompted this, our standpoint on the problem of religion
will undergo a marked shift. We tell ourselves how
lovely it would be, would it not, if there were a God
who created the universe and benign Providence, a
moral world order, and life beyond the grave, yet it is

very evident, is it not, that all of this is the way we should inevitably wish it to be. And it would be even more remarkable if our poor, ignorant bondsman ancestors had managed to solve all these difficult cosmic questions.

Very evident, isn't that: that all of this is, by way of thought, unavoidably won; it is so. And it would be even more convincing if...

VII

Having acknowledged that the teachings of religion are illusions, the further question immediately arises: are not other parts of our cultural inheritance, parts that we hold in high esteem and allow to dominate our lives, of a similar nature? Could it be that the premises governing our state institutions must likewise be termed illusions, could it be that relations between the genders in our culture are clouded by one or a number of erotic illusions? Our misgivings once aroused, we shall not even shrink from asking whether our own conviction (that by applying observation and thinking in scientific work we can learn something of external reality) is any more firmly grounded. Nothing must be allowed to prevent us from approving the application of observation to our own being and the use of thinking in the service of its own critique. A series of investigations opens up here, the outcome of which would inevitably have a crucial effect on the structure of a 'way of viewing the world'. We also sense that the effort will not be wasted and that it will at least partially justify our suspicion. However, the author's competence balks at so huge a task; he has no choice but to confine his essay to tracing just one of those illusions – that of religion.

Here our opponent shouts '*Stop!*' We are about to be called to account for our forbidden conduct. This is what he tells us: '*Archaeological interests are entirely laudable, no doubt, but no one starts an excavation if it is going to undermine the dwellings of the living, making them collapse and burying people under the rubble. The teachings of religion are not just another object to be pored over. Our culture is based on them, it is a condition of the preservation of human society that the vast majority of people believes in the truth of those teachings. If people are taught that there is no all-powerful, all-righteous God, no divine world order, and no life after death, they will feel under no obligation to obey the rules of culture. Everyone will follow his anti-social, egoistical drives without fear or inhibition, seeking to assert his power; the chaos that we banished through many millennia of cultural endeavour will return. Even if it were known and could be proved that religion is not in possession of the truth, nothing must be said and people should behave in the way that the "as if" philosophy requires. In the interests of everyone's preservation! Also, apart from the danger of the enterprise, it constitutes pointless cruelty. Innumerable human beings find no other consolation than the teachings of religion; only with their aid do such folk find life bearable. An attempt is being made to rob them of that support without giving them anything better in its place. Admittedly, science has not come up with much so far, but even if it was a great deal more advanced it would not satisfy the human race. A person has other impera- tive needs that cold science can never meet, and it is a very strange thing (indeed, the pinnacle of inconsistency) that a psychologist who has always stressed by how much, in human existence, intelligence takes second place to the driven life, should now proceed to deprive people of a precious piece of wish-fulfilment and seek to compensate them with intellectual fare instead.'*

So many accusations, one on top of another! However, I am ready to rebut them all, added to which I shall be putting forward the view that culture is at greater risk if its present attitude towards religion is maintained than if that attitude is abandoned. The trouble is, I hardly know where to begin with my refutation.

Possibly with the assurance that I myself see my undertaking as entirely harmless and risk-free. Overrating the intellect is not on my side this time. If people are as my opponent describes them (and I have no wish to disagree), there is no danger of a pious believer, overwhelmed by my arguments, allowing his faith to be wrested from him. Furthermore, I have said nothing that other, better men have not said far more comprehensively, powerfully and impressively before me. The names of those men are well known; I shall not cite them lest I make it look as if I am trying to place myself in their line of descent. All I have done (this is the only new element in my account) is to add a certain amount of psychological justification to the criticisms put forward by my great predecessors. This particular addition can scarcely be expected to force an issue that earlier writers failed to effect. I could of course be asked at this point: why write such things when you are confident they will achieve nothing? But we shall come back to that later.

The only person this publication may harm is myself. I shall be treated to the most unpleasant accusations of shallowness, bigotry, lack of idealism and want of sympathy for the highest interests of the human race. However, on the one hand such reproaches are nothing new so far as I am concerned; on the other, when a man has already risen above the displeasure of his contemporaries in younger years, why should it bother him in extreme old age, when he is sure of soon being beyond all favour and disfavour? In the past it was different, such remarks were certain to earn one a curtailment of one's earthly existence and a greatly accelerated opportunity of gaining personal experience of the afterlife. I repeat, however: those times are gone, and today writing such things entails no danger, even so far as the author is concerned. The worst that can happen is that the book is not translated and may not be distributed in one country or another. Not of course in a country that feels confident of the high standing of its culture. But if, in general, one is advocating wish-renunciation and surrender to one's fate, even these losses must be borne.

It then occurred to me to wonder whether publication of this essay might not after all do some damage. Not to a person, granted, but to a thing – namely, the cause of psychoanalysis. The fact is, there is no denying that it is my creation, people have shown plenty of mistrust and ill-will towards it; if I now come out with such unwelcome remarks, they will be only too ready to make the shift, the 'displacement', from my person to psychoanalysis. Now, they will say, we see what psychoanalysis leads to. The mask is off; to a denial of God and the moral ideal, just as we always suspected. To stop us finding out, we were offered the pretence that psychoanalysis, allegedly, has no particular world-view, nor is it capable of forming one.

Such an outcry will be genuinely regrettable so far as I am concerned, because of my many colleagues, some of whom do not begin to share my stance on religious problems. However, psychoanalysis has already withstood many storms and must weather this new one too. In reality, psychoanalysis is a method of research, an impartial tool – like, say, infinitesimal calculus. If a physicist should use the latter to work out that, after a certain time, the earth will perish, people will nevertheless hesitate to ascribe destructive tendencies to the calculus itself and outlaw it accordingly. Everything I have said here against the truth-value of religions did not need psychoanalysis, it had been said by others long before psychoanalysis came about. If applying psychoanalytic method can furnish a fresh argument against the truth content of religion, *tant pis* for religion, but defenders of religion are equally entitled to use psychoanalysis to do full justice to the affective significance of religious doctrine.

Right, to proceed with the defence: religion has clearly done human culture great services, it has contributed much to taming anti-social drives, but not enough. For many thousands of years it has dominated human society; it has had time to show what it can do. Had it succeeded in making the majority of human beings happy, in comforting them, reconciling them to life, turning them into upholders of culture, no one would even think of trying to change the way things are. What do we see instead? That an alarmingly large number of people are dissatisfied with culture and unhappy within it, they experience it as a yoke that needs to be thrown off, we see that those people either devote their whole strength to changing that culture or take their hostility to it to such lengths as to refuse to have anything at all to do with culture and the curbing of drives. Here it will be objected that this state of affairs in fact came about because religion had lost some of its influence over the mass of the people – precisely because of the regrettable effect of scientific advances. We shall note the admission, together with the reasons given for it, and use it later for our own purposes, but the objection itself has no force.

It is doubtful whether, at the time when religious teachings held unrestricted sway, the human race was happier, by and large, than it is today; it was certainly no more moral. People have always known how to trivialize the rules of religion, thereby thwarting their intention. Priests, whose role it was to monitor obedience to religion, helped them in this. God's goodness inevitably spiked the guns of his righteousness, as it were: people sinned, then they made sacrifice or did penance, then they were free to sin again. Russian inwardness contrived to reach the conclusion that sin was indispensable to an enjoyment of all the blessings of God's grace; at bottom, therefore, it was pleasing in the sight of God. Obviously the only way priests could keep the bulk of the people submissive to religion was by making such vast concessions to human libidinal nature. The fact remained: God alone is strong and good; humans, by contrast, are weak and sinful. Immorality has always, in every age, found quite as much support in religion as has morality. If the achievements of religion in relation to making people happy, fitting them to culture, and reining them in morally are not better than they are, then surely we must ask: do we overrate its essentialness for humanity and are we wise to base our cultural requirements on it?

Consider the situation that unmistakably obtains today. We heard the admission that religion no longer has the same influence over people as was once the case. (The culture at issue here is European Christendom.) Not because its promises have become more modest but because people find those promises less credible. Let us concede that the reason for the change is the strengthening of the scientific mind in the upper strata of human society. (This may not be the only reason.) Criticism has nibbled away at the evidential value of religious documents, the natural sciences have exposed the errors they contain, comparative research has noticed an embarrassing similarity between the religious ideas to which we pay tribute and the spiritual productions of primitive peoples and eras.

The scientific mind generates a specific way of approaching the things of this world; faced with the things of religion, it pauses, hesitates, and finally here too steps over the threshold. The process is unstoppable, the more people have access to the treasures of our knowledge, the more widespread the severance from religious belief – at first only from the outdated, offensive fashions in which it is kitted out, but then also from its fundamental premises. The Americans who conducted the monkey trial in Dayton are the only ones who have shown consistency.[1] Usually, the inevitable transition takes place through the medium of half-truths and insincerities.

Culture has little to fear from educated persons and those who work with their intellect. The replacement of religious motives for cultural behaviour by other, secular ones would in their case proceed in silence; moreover, they are themselves for the most part upholders of culture. It is different with the great mass of the uneducated and oppressed, who have every reason to be hostile to culture. Provided they do not find out that God is no longer believed in, all is well. But they will find out, they are bound to, even if this essay of mine remains unpublished. And they are ready to accept the results of scientific thinking without there having taken place within them the change that scientific thinking occasions in people. When they do, is there not a risk that the hostility of those masses to culture will pounce on the weak point that they have spotted in the system that keeps them in check? If your only reason for not striking your neighbour dead is that the good Lord forbade it and will punish it severely in this life or the next, but you then learn that there is no good Lord and no need to fear his chastisement, you are going to strike him or her dead without scruple, and only some earthly power will be able to prevent you from doing so. In which case

[1] [Two years earlier (1925), in Dayton, Tennessee, a biology teacher had been found guilty of teaching evolution. The so-called 'Monkey Trial' of 1925 focused opposition between those who accepted the ideas of Charles Darwin and the 'Creationists' of Christian fundamentalism.]

the alternatives are: unrelenting oppression of those dangerous masses, coupled with very careful blocking of all opportunities for intellectual awakening, or a thorough review of the relationship between culture and religion.

VIII

One would think that no particular difficulties stood in the way of implementing this latter proposal. Granted, it means giving something up, but the gain may be greater and a big risk is avoided. However, people shrink from such a step, as if culture would be exposed to an even bigger risk. When St Boniface chopped down the tree that the Saxons worshipped as sacred, onlookers expected some dreadful event to follow the crime. It did not supervene, and the Saxons accepted baptism.

When culture established the ban on killing the neighbour whom one dislikes personally, who is in the way, or whose goods arouse envy, clearly this occurred in the interests of human coexistence, which would not otherwise be feasible. The reason for this is that the murderer would attract the vengeance of the relatives of the murdered person and the vague jealousy of others who felt an equal inner inclination to commit such violence; in other words, he would not enjoy his revenge or his robbery for long but would have every prospect of soon being done to death in his turn. Even were he to protect himself against the individual enemy by exceptional strength and wariness, he would inevitably be subdued by a league of weaker foes. If no such league emerged, the killing would continue unchecked with the end result that the human race wiped itself out. The same state of affairs would exist between individuals as still exists between families in Corsica but elsewhere only between nations. The risk of physical insecurity, which is the same for all, has the effect of uniting human beings in a society that forbids the individual to kill and reserves the right collectively to kill whoever violates the ban. It is called justice and punishment.

However, this rational explanation of the ban on murder is not the one we give; we claim that God enacted the ban. In other words, we dare to guess his intentions, and we find that he too does not want human beings to wipe one another out. In acting in this way, we clothe the cultural ban in very special solemnity, yet in the process we risk making observance of it dependent on belief in God. If we undo that step, no longer shifting what we want on to God but contenting ourselves with the social explanation, we shall have abandoned that transfiguration of the cultural ban, true, but we shall also have avoided placing it at risk. However, we make another gain as well. Through a kind of diffusion or infection, the character of holiness or inviolability (other-worldliness, one might almost say) has spread from a few major bans to all other cultural institutions, laws and ordinances. On these, however, a halo often does not sit well. It is not simply that they devalue one another by reaching conflicting decisions at different times and in different places; they also display every sign of human inadequacy. It is easy to recognize among them what may simply be a product of a myopic anxiety, the expression of petty interests, or a conclusion drawn from inadequate premises. The criticism to which they will inevitably be subjected also (and to an undesirable extent) reduces respect for other, more justified cultural requirements. It is a difficult task, deciding what God himself required and what is more likely to stem from the authority of an all-powerful parliament or lofty magistrate. So it would be an undoubted advantage to leave God out of it altogether and frankly concede the purely human origin of all cultural institutions and rules. Along with the holiness to which they lay claim, the rigidity and immutability of such commandments and laws would also fall away. People would be able to understand that such precepts had been created not so much to keep them under control, rather to serve their interests; they would gain a more cordial attitude towards them, seeking less to overturn them, more to improve them. This would be an important step along the road leading to a reconciliation with the pressures of culture.

At this point, however, our plea in favour of basing rules of culture on purely rational grounds, i.e. tracing them back to social necessity, is cut short by a scruple. We took as our example the origin of the ban on murder. In which case, does our account match the historical truth? We fear it does not; it appears to be a mere intellectual construct. Having made a particular study of this part of human cultural history with the aid of psychoanalysis, on the basis of that endeavour we are obliged to say that in reality things were different. Purely rational motives achieve little against passionate impulses, even in people nowadays; how much less effective must they have been in connection with the human animal of primeval times! Possibly the latter's descendants would still be uninhibitedly mowing one another down had there not, amongst those murderous deeds, been one, namely the striking dead of the primal father, that had elicited an irresistible emotional reaction involving momentous consequences. That is the origin of the 'you shall not kill' commandment, which in totemism was confined to the father-substitute; extended subsequently to include others, it is still not universally enforced today.

However, as I explain elsewhere (so there is no need for me to repeat those remarks here), that primal father was the primitive image of God, the model on which subsequent generations based the figure of the deity. So the religious account is correct: God really was involved in the origin of the ban; it was his influence, not any understanding of social necessity, that created it. And the displacement of human will on to God is wholly legitimate; men knew that they had violently removed their father, and in reaction to the crime they resolved henceforth to respect his will. Religious teaching is telling us the historical truth, albeit with an element of distortion and disguise; our rational account is a denial of it.

Here we become aware that the treasure-house of religious ideas does not contain wish-fulfilments alone but also significant historical reminiscences. What matchless power it must bestow upon religion, combining the forces of past and future in this way! But possibly, with the aid of an analogy, we can glimpse a different view. It is not a good idea to transplant concepts a long way away from the soil in which they have grown, but this correspondence must be voiced. We know that the human child has difficulty in making the transformation to culture without passing through a more or less clear period of neurosis. The reason for this is that the child is unable to suppress many of the subsequently unusable drive-demands by rational intellectual effort but must curb them through acts of repression, the usual motive behind which is fear. Most of these childhood neuroses are spontaneously overcome as the child grows up; this is particularly the fate of the obsessional neuroses of childhood. As for the rest, psychoanalytical treatment in later life is supposed to clear those up too. In an entirely analogous manner, one might assume that, during its centuries-long evolution, the human race as a whole gets into states that are like neuroses – and for the same reasons, namely because in the eras when it languished in ignorance and was intellectually weak it produced the drive-renunciations essential to human coexistence through purely affective forces alone. The fall-out from quasi-repressive processes occurring in primeval times clung to culture for a long time to come. Religion, in this reading, is the universal human obsessional neurosis; like the child's, it stemmed from the Oedipus complex, the relationship to the father. Accordingly, a turning away from religion must be expected to occur with the fateful inexorability of a growth process, and we (in this view) are in the throes of that phase of evolution right now.

So our behaviour should be modelled on that of an understanding teacher, who rather than resisting an imminent transformation seeks to promote it while curbing the violence of its breakthrough. However, the analogy does not exhaust the essence of religion. If on the one hand it brings obsessional restrictions such as only an individual obsessional neurosis can do, on the other hand it contains a system of wish-illusions coupled with a denial of reality such as we find in isolation only in amentia, a happy state of hallucinatory confusion. The fact is, these are only comparisons, with the aid of which we are struggling to understand the social phenomenon; the pathology of the individual provides us with no fully adequate equivalent.

It has been pointed out repeatedly (by myself and in particular by Theodor Reik) to what level of detail analogies of religion with obsessional neurosis can be pursued and how much of the particularities and destinies of the emergence of religion can be understood in this way. Another good thing is that the devout believer is to a great extent protected from the risk of certain neurotic ailments; adoption of the universal neurosis relieves him of the task of cultivating a personal neurosis.

Acknowledging the historical value of certain religious teachings increases our respect for them but does not invalidate our proposal to remove them as a motivating force behind the rules of culture. Quite the contrary! It is thanks to these historical residues, in fact, that our view of religious dogmas as quasi-neurotic relics has arisen, and now we can say that it is probably time, as in the analytic treatment of the neurotic, for the results of repression to be replaced by the outcomes of ratiocination. That such reworking will not stop at renunciation of the solemn transfiguration of the rules of culture, that a general revision of the same will inevitably, for many people, lead to their being repealed – these things are to be expected but scarcely to be regretted. That is how our appointed task (that of reconciling people with culture) will to a great extent be resolved. We need make no apology for departing from historical truth in providing a rational motivation for the rules of culture. The truths contained in the teachings of religion are so distorted and systematically dressed up that the mass of humanity is incapable of recognizing them as truth. It is not unlike the way we tell children that babies are brought by the stork. That too is a way of telling the truth in symbolic disguise, because we know what the big bird stands for. But the child does not know, all it hears is the element of distortion, it feels cheated, and we know how often children's distrust of adults and the child's contrariness spring from just such an impression. We have reached the conclusion that it is better to stop handing down such symbolic obfuscations of the truth and refusing to provide the child, in a manner appropriate to its stage of intellectual development, with a knowledge of the way things really are.

IX

'You indulge yourself in contradictions that are difficult to reconcile. First you claim that an essay such as yours is entirely harmless. No one is going to let himself be robbed of his religious belief by such remarks. But since, as we shall see, you do in fact mean to shake that belief, the question legitimately arises: so why publish it? Elsewhere, however, you concede that some harm (much harm, even) may indeed be done if someone discovers that God is no longer believed in. Hitherto obedient, that person will now cast obedience to the rules of culture aside. The fact is, your whole argument that the religious motivation of cultural commands constitutes a danger to culture depends on the assumption that the believer can be turned into a non-believer, and that, surely, is a complete contradiction?

'Another contradiction is when you concede on the one hand that human beings cannot be guided by intelligence, they are in thrall to their passions and libidinal demands, but propose on the other hand that the affective foundations of their cultural obedience be replaced by rational ones. What is that all about? To my mind, it is either one thing or the other.

'Anyway, have you learned nothing from history? A similar attempt to have reason supersede religion has been made before

– officially and on a grand scale. Don't you remember the
French Revolution and Robespierre? And don't you also
remember how ephemeral and miserably unsuccessful the
experiment was? It is currently being repeated in Russia, no
need to ask how it will turn out this time. Surely we can
assume that human beings cannot get by without religion?

'You say yourself that religion is more than an obsessional
neurosis. Yet you do not discuss this other aspect. You are
content to run through the analogy with neurosis. It is a
neurosis that humanity needs freeing from. You are not
bothered what else gets lost in the process.'

Probably the appearance of contradiction came about
because I was dealing with complicated matters in too
great a hurry. Some things we can go over again. I still
maintain that in one respect my essay is quite harmless.
No believer is going to allow his faith to be shaken
by these or similar arguments. A believer has specific
emotional attachments to the content of religion. There
are doubtless innumerable others who do not believe in
the same way. They obey the rules of culture because
they let themselves be intimidated by the threats of
religion, and they fear religion all the while they are
required to treat it as part of the reality placing restrictions upon them. These are the people who break out
as soon as they are allowed to stop believing in the
reality-value of religion, but again this is something that
arguments do not influence. Such people cease to fear
religion once they become aware that others too are not
afraid of it, and they were the object of my claim that
the decline of religious influence would come to their
attention even were I not to publish my essay.

However, I believe you yourself attach greater importance to the other contradiction with which you reproach me. Humans, you say, are scarcely amenable to rational motives, they are wholly in thrall to their libidinal desires. So why deprive them of a libidinal satisfaction and seek to replace it with rational motives? Granted, humans are like that, but have you ever asked yourself whether they need to be, whether their innermost nature demands it? Is the anthropologist able to supply the cranial index of a tribe that practises the custom of deforming its children's little heads with bandages from an early age? Think of the distressing contrast between the radiant intelligence of a healthy child and the intellectual feebleness of the average adult. Is it not at least possible that in fact religious education is largely to blame for this relative atrophy? I believe it would be a very long time before an uninfluenced child began spontaneously to have thoughts about God and matters beyond this world. It could be that such thoughts would then follow the same path as in the case of the child's ancestors. Yet no one waits for this to happen; the child is fed the teachings of religion at a time when it is neither interested in them nor able to grasp their scope. Pushing back sexual development and bringing forward the influence of religion – those are the top two programmatic aims of modern pedagogics, are they not? So when the child's mind awakes, the teachings of religion have already become untouchable. But do you suppose it is particularly conducive to strengthening the intellectual function that so important an area should be closed off to it by the threat of hellfire? Once a person has persuaded himself to accept uncritically all the absurdities that the teachings of religion heap upon him and even to overlook the contradictions between them, we need not be too surprised to find him intellectually enfeebled. But we have no means of controlling our libidinal nature apart from our intelligence. How can people dominated by intellectual prohibitions be expected to attain the psychological ideal of the primacy of the intelligence? You will also be aware that women in general are accused of so-called 'physiological feebleness of mind', i.e. of being less intelligent than men. The fact itself is in dispute and its interpretation questionable, but one argument for the secondary nature of such intellectual atrophy is that women suffer from the harshness of the early ban on directing their thoughts towards what they would have been most interested in, namely the problems of sex life. As long as, in addition to the sexual mental block, the religious mental block and the loyal block derived therefrom operate on a person's early years, we really cannot say what that person is really like.

However, I am prepared to moderate my zeal and admit the possibility that I too am chasing an illusion. Maybe the effect of the religious ban on thought is not as bad as I am assuming; it may turn out that human nature remains the same even if education is not abused to induce subservience to religion. I do not know, nor can you know that yourself. Not only do the greatest problems of this life currently seem insoluble; many lesser questions are also difficult to decide. But grant me this much: there are grounds for hope here as regards the future, a treasure may lie buried here by which culture may be enriched, it is worth the effort of experimenting with a non-religious education. If the outcome is unsatisfactory, I am prepared to abandon reform and go back to the earlier, purely descriptive verdict: humans are creatures of feeble intelligence, dominated by their libidinal desires.

On another point I agree with you wholeheartedly. It is certainly a nonsensical plan to seek to abolish religion by force and at a stroke. Principally because there is no chance of its succeeding. The believer will not allow his faith to be taken from him – not by arguments and not by bans. If in a few cases this was in fact achieved, it would be an act of cruelty. A person who has for decades taken a sleeping draught will of course be unable to sleep when deprived of the draught. That the effect of the consolations of religion can be likened to that of a narcotic is neatly illustrated by something happening in America. There an attempt is currently being made (clearly under the influence of matriarchy) to deprive people of all stimulants, drugs and semi-luxuries and sate them, by way of recompense, with the fear of God. The outcome of this experiment is another thing over which we need squander no curiosity.

So I take issue with you when you go on to infer that people cannot do without the consolation of the religious illusion at all, that without it they could not bear the burden of life, could not tolerate cruel reality. No, they could not – those to whom you have been administering the sweet (or bittersweet) poison since childhood. But what about the others, who have been brought up rationally? Perhaps a person not suffering from the neurosis needs no intoxicant to ease it. Granted, such a person will then be in a difficult position, he will have to admit that he is completely helpless, insignificant amid the world's bustle, no longer the mid-point of creation, no longer the object of tender care on the part of a benign Providence. He will be in the same situation as the child who has left the home where it had felt so warm and cosy. But surely infantilism is something that is meant to be overcome? A person cannot remain a child for ever; eventually the child must go out into what has been called 'hostile life'. The process might be termed *'education for reality'*. Do you still need me to make plain to you that the sole object of my essay is to draw attention to the necessity for this step forward?

You are afraid, probably, that people will not survive the ordeal. Well, we can only hope they will. It certainly makes a difference, knowing that one is dependent on one's own strength. A person learns, then, to make proper use of that strength. Humans are not entirely without succour, their science has taught them much since the ice age and will extend their power even further. And as for the great exigencies of fate, against which there is no recourse, they will simply learn to bear them with humility. Of what use to them is the pretence of some great estate on the moon, from the yield of which no one has actually seen a penny as yet? An honest peasant here on this earth will know how to farm his patch in such a way that it feeds him. By withdrawing his expectations from the beyond and concentrating all the forces thus released on earthly existence, he will doubtless manage to make life bearable for all and ensure that culture quite ceases to oppress. Then he will be able, without regret, to echo the words of one of our fellow unbelievers:

> Den Himmel überlassen wir
> Den Engeln und den Spatzen.

[Let us leave the heavens to angels and to sparrows.]

X

'That sounds splendid, I have to say. A human race that, having dispensed with all illusions, has become capable of managing tolerably on earth! However, I cannot share your expectations. Not because I am the stubborn reactionary for whom you perhaps take me. No, from level-headedness. I believe we have exchanged roles: you now come across as the enthusiast who allows himself to be carried away by illusions, while I represent the claims of reason, the right to scepticism. What you have been saying seems to me to be based on errors that, following your own procedure, I may term illusions because they so clearly reveal the influence of your desires. You set your hopes on generations uninfluenced by religious teachings in early childhood easily attaining your longed-for goal of the primacy of intelligence over the libidinal life. That is an illusion if ever there was one; on this crucial point human nature is unlikely to change. If I am not mistaken (one knows so little about other cultures), even today there are nations that do not grow up under the pressure of a religious system, and they come no closer to your ideal than do others. If you want to abolish religion from our European culture, that can only happen as a result of a different doctrinal system, and from the outset that system would assume, in its own defence, all the psychological characteristics of religion, the same *sanctity, rigidity, intolerance, the same ban on thought. You have to have something of the kind to meet the requirements of education. Education itself is something you cannot dispense with. The road from infant to civilized being is a long one; too many of our weaker brethren would lose their way along it and fail to accomplish their life's work in time if left to develop on their own, without guidance. The teachings employed in their education will always set limits to the thinking of their more mature years, precisely as you accuse religion of doing today. Can you not see that it is the irredeemable congenital defect of our culture, of every culture, that it asks the compulsive, intellectually feeble child to make decisions that only the mature intelligence of the adult can justify? Yet it cannot do otherwise, given the condensation of centuries of human development into a few childhood years, and only affective forces can make the child cope with its appointed task. That is what your 'primacy of the intelligence' can look forward to.*

'So you should not be surprised if I speak up for retaining the system of religious teaching as basis for education and human coexistence. It is a practical problem, not a question of reality-value. Since, in the interests of preserving our culture, we cannot put off influencing the individual until he has become culturally mature (many individuals would never be that), since we are compelled to impose on the younger generation some system of teachings aimed at having upon them the effect of a premise that is beyond criticism, the religious system strikes me as being by far the most suitable one for the job. Precisely, of course, because of its wish-fulfilling, consoling power, which you claim to have recognized as an "illusion". Given the problems associated with discerning something of

reality (indeed, the doubtfulness of our being able to do so at all), let us not forget that human needs, too, form part of reality – and an important part at that, one that is of particular concern to us.

'I find a further advantage of religious doctrine in a feature of it that appears to cause you especial offence. It permits a conceptual purification and sublimation that make it possible to strip away most of what bears traces of primitive and infantile thinking. We are left with a body of ideas that science no longer contradicts and is unable to refute. These rearrangements of religious doctrine, which you condemn as half-measures and compromises, make it possible to avoid a split between the uneducated mass and the philosophical thinker; they preserve the common ground between them that is so important as regards safeguarding culture. There is then no fear of the man in the street discovering that the upper strata of society "no longer believe in God". I think I have demonstrated now that your efforts boil down to an attempt to replace one tried and tested, affectively precious illusion by another that is untried and unsophisticated.'

I would not have you think I am deaf to your criticisms. I know how hard it is to avoid illusions; the hopes I have professed may indeed themselves be illusory in nature. But one difference I insist on. My illusions (apart from the fact that no punishment attaches to not sharing them) are not unalterable, as are those of religion, they lack that manic character. Should experience reveal (not to me but to others after me who think as I do) that we have made a mistake, we shall drop our expectations. Please, take my attempt for what it is. A psychologist who is well aware of how difficult it is to cope with life in this world is endeavouring to assess the development of humanity on the basis of the scrap of understanding that he has acquired from studying the mental processes of the individual as that individual evolves from being a child to being an adult. In the process, the view forces itself upon him that religion is like a childhood neurosis, and he is optimistic enough to assume that the human race will conquer this neurotic phase, as so many children outgrow their similar neurosis. These insights from individual psychology may be inadequate, transferring them to the human race as a whole may be unjustified, such optimism may be baseless; I own up to all these uncertainties. But one often cannot help saying what one thinks, one's excuse being that no more is claimed for the pronouncement than it is worth.

And there are two points I need to dwell on a little. Firstly, the weakness of my position in no way implies a strengthening of your own. I believe you to be defending a lost cause. Never mind how often we repeat (and rightly so) that the human intellect is powerless in comparison with human drives, there remains something special about that weakness; the voice of the intellect is a low one, yet it does not cease until it has gained a hearing. In the end, after countless rejections, it does so. This is one of the few respects in which one may be optimistic for the future of the human race, but as such it is not without importance. Other hopes can be hitched to it. The primacy of the intellect undoubtedly lies in the far, far distant but probably not infinitely distant future. And since it may be expected to set itself the same goals as you expect your God to realize (on a reduced, human scale, of course, i.e. so far as external reality or Ἀνάγκη allows), namely human love and the limitation of suffering, we can tell each other that our opposition is only temporary; it is not irreconcilable. We hope for the same things, but you are in more of a hurry, are more demanding, and (why not come out with it?) more self-interested than myself and my associates. You want to have bliss begin immediately after death, you demand the impossible of it, you refuse to surrender the claims of the individual. Of those desires, our god Λόγος ['reason'] will grant what nature (apart from ourselves) permits, but very gradually, only in the unforeseeable future and for fresh generations. A reward for ourselves, who suffer grievously from life, is not among his promises. On the way to that distant goal your religious teachings will have to be dropped, regardless of whether the first experiments miscarry, regardless of whether the first substitutions prove unfounded. You know why; ultimately, nothing can withstand reason and experience, and the fact that religion contradicts both is all too tangible. Not even reformed religious ideas, where they nevertheless seek to salvage something of religion's consolation content, can escape this fate. Of course, if they confine themselves to proclaiming a superior spiritual essence whose properties are indeterminable and whose purposes are unknowable, they will be safe from the objections of science, but they will also, in that case, be abandoned by the interest of humankind.

And secondly: look at the difference between our respective attitudes to illusion. You need to defend the religious illusion with all your might; if it is invalidated (and it really is pretty much under threat), your world collapses and you are left with no alternative but to despair of everything, of culture and of the future of the human race. I – we – know no such thraldom. Being ready to relinquish a large part of our infantile desires, we can stand it if a few of our expectations turn out to be illusions.

Freed from the pressure of religious teachings, education may not do much to change people's psychological value. Our god may not be Λόγος particularly omnipotent, not able to perform more than a fraction of what his predecessors promised. If we have to concede this, we shall do so with humility. It is not going to make us lose interest in the world and in life, because at one point we have a solid underpinning that you lack. We believe it is possible for the work of science to discover something of the reality of the world, as a result of which we shall be able to increase our power and in accordance with which we shall be able to arrange our lives. If that belief is an illusion, then we are in the same position as yourself, but science has given us proof, in the shape of a great many significant successes, that it is no illusion. Science has numerous overt and even more covert enemies among those who cannot forgive it for having weakened religious faith and for threatening to overthrow it. Those enemies say accusingly how little science has taught us and how very much more (incomparably more) it has shed no light on whatsoever. But they forget how young it is, how difficult were its beginnings, and for how immeasurably brief a time the human intellect has possessed the strength for the tasks of science. Do we not all make the mistake of basing our judgements on time-spans that are too short? We should follow the geologists' example. People complain of the uncertainty of science, pointing to the fact that today it promulgates as law something that the next generation acknowledges to have been an error, substituting a fresh law, which then enjoys an equally brief period of validity. But that is unfair and in part untrue. Changes of scientific opinion constitute development and progress, not upheaval. A law that was initially seen as having total validity turns out to be a special case of a more comprehensive regularity or is curbed by a different law that is discovered only later; a rough approximation to the truth is replaced by one that is more precisely adapted – which in turn looks forward to a more perfect adjustment. In various fields, a research phase has yet to be outgrown in which assumptions are tested that soon need to be rejected as inadequate; in others, an assured and virtually unalterable core of knowledge already exists. Endless attempts have been made radically to devalue the scientific endeavour by suggesting that, because it is tied to the conditions of our own organization, it cannot help but furnish only subjective findings, while the real nature of things outside ourselves remains beyond its reach. However, this is to disregard a number of factors crucial to the perception of scientific work: that our organization (i.e. our mental apparatus) was in fact developed in the effort to map the outside world, so must have realized a certain amount of expediency in its structure; that that apparatus is itself a part of the world we set out to investigate and very much admits such investigation;

that the task of science is described in full if we limit it to showing how, because of our unique organization, the world must inevitably appear to us; that the eventual results of science, precisely because of the manner of their acquisition, are conditioned not only by our organization but also by what influenced that organization; and lastly that the problem of a world constitution that takes no account of the mental apparatus by which we perceive it is an empty abstraction, of no practical interest.

No, our science is not an illusion. What would be an illusion would be to think we might obtain elsewhere that which science cannot give us.

(1927)

Mourning and Melancholia

Dreams having served us as the normal model for narciss-istic mental disorders, we shall now attempt to cast some light on the nature of melancholia by comparing it to the normal affect of mourning. This time, though, we must begin our account with an admission which should warn us against overestimating our conclusions. Melan-cholia, the definition of which fluctuates even in des-criptive psychiatry, appears in various different clinical forms; these do not seem amenable to being grouped together into a single entity, and some of them suggest somatic rather than psychogenetic diseases. Apart from those impressions that are available to any observer, our material is restricted to a small number of cases whose psychogenetic nature was beyond a doubt. We shall therefore relinquish all claim to the universal validity of our results, and console ourselves by reflecting that with the means of investigation presently at our disposal we could hardly find something that was not typical, if not of a whole class of illnesses, then at least of a smaller group.

The correlation between melancholia and mourn-ing seems justified by the overall picture of the two conditions. Further, the causes of both in terms of environmental influences are, where we can identify them at all, also the same. Mourning is commonly the reaction to the loss of a beloved person or an abstraction taking the place of the person, such as fatherland, freedom, an ideal and so on. In some people, whom we for this reason suspect of having a pathological disposition, melancholia appears in place of mourning. It is also most remarkable that it never occurs to us to consider mourning as a pathological condition and present it to the doctor for treatment, despite the fact that it produces severe deviations from normal behaviour. We rely on it being overcome after a certain period of time, and consider interfering with it to be pointless, or even damaging.

Melancholia is mentally characterized by a profoundly painful depression, a loss of interest in the outside world, the loss of the ability to love, the inhibition of any kind of performance and a reduction in the sense of self, expressed in self-recrimination and self-directed insults, intensifying into the delusory expectation of punishment. We have a better understanding of this when we bear in mind that mourning displays the same traits, apart from one: the disorder of self-esteem is absent. In all other respects, however, it is the same. Serious mourning, the reaction to the loss of a loved one, contains the same painful mood, the loss of interest in the outside world – except as it recalls the deceased – the loss of ability to choose any new love-object – which would mean replacing the mourned one – turning away from any task that is not related to the memory of the deceased. We can easily understand that this inhibition and restriction of the ego is a manifestation of exclusive devotion to mourning, leaving nothing over for other interests and intentions. The only reason, in fact, why this behaviour does not strike us as pathological is that we are so easily able to explain it.

We also endorse the comparison that identifies the mood of mourning as a 'painful' one. Its justification will probably be clear to us when we are capable of providing an economical characterization of pain.

So what is the work that mourning performs? I do not think I am stretching a point if I present it in the following manner: reality-testing has revealed that the beloved object no longer exists, and demands that the libido as a whole sever its bonds with that object. An understandable tendency arises to counter this – it may be generally observed that people are reluctant to abandon a libido position, even if a substitute is already beckoning. This tendency can become so intense that it leads to a person turning away from reality and holding on to the object through a hallucinatory wish-psychosis (see the essay ['Metapsychological Complement to Dream Theory']). Normally, respect for reality carries the day. But its task cannot be accomplished immediately. It is now carried out piecemeal at great expenditure of time and investment of energy, and the lost object persists in the psyche. Each individual memory and expectation in which the libido was connected to the object is adjusted and hyper-invested, leading to its detachment from the libido. Why this compromise enforcement of the reality commandment, which is carried out piece by piece, should be so extraordinarily painful is not at all easy to explain in economic terms. It is curious that this pain-unpleasure strikes us as natural. In fact, the ego is left free and uninhibited once again after the mourning-work is completed.

Let us now apply to melancholia what we have learned from mourning. In a large number of cases it is clear that it too may be a reaction to the loss of a beloved object; when other causes are present, it may be possible to recognize that the loss is more notional in nature. The object may not really have died, for example, but may instead have been lost as a love-object (as, for example, in the case of an abandoned bride). In yet other cases we think that we should cling to our assumption of such a loss, but it is difficult to see what has been lost, so we may rather assume that the patient cannot consciously grasp what he has lost. Indeed, this might also be the case when the loss that is the cause of the melancholia is known to the subject, when he knows *who* it is, but not *what* it is about that person that he has lost. So the obvious thing is for us somehow to relate melancholia to the loss of an object that is withdrawn from consciousness, unlike mourning, in which no aspect of the loss is unconscious.

In the case of mourning, we found that inhibition and apathy were fully explained by the absorption of the ego in the mourning-work. The unknown loss in the case of melancholia will also lead to similar internal work, and will consequently be responsible for the inhibition of melancholia. But melancholic inhibition seems puzzling to us because we are unable to see what it is that so completely absorbs the patient. There is one other aspect of melancholia that is absent from mourning, an extra-ordinary reduction in self-esteem, a great impoverishment of the ego. In mourning, the world has become poor and empty, in melancholia it is the ego that has become so. The patient describes his ego to us as being worthless, incapable of functioning and morally reprehensible, he is filled with self-reproach, he levels insults against himself and expects ostracism and punishment. He abases himself before everyone else, he feels sorry for those close to him for being connected to such an unworthy person. He does not sense that a change has taken place in him, but extends his self-criticism to cover the past; he asserts that he has never been any better. The image of this – predominantly moral – sense of inferiority is complemented by sleeplessness, rejection of food, and an overcoming of the drive – most curious from the psychological point of view – which compels everything that lives to cling to life.

It would be fruitless both from the scientific and the therapeutic point of view to contradict the patient who levels such reproaches against his ego in this way. In all likelihood he must in some way be right, and must be describing a state of affairs as it appears to him. Indeed, we must immediately confirm some of his information straight away. He really is as apathetic, as incapable of love and achievement as he says he is. But that, as we know, is secondary, it is the consequence of the internal work, unknown to us and comparable to mourning, that is devouring his ego. He also seems to us to be right in some of his other self-reproaches, and only to be grasping the truth more keenly than others who are not

melancholic. If, intensifying his self-criticism, he describes himself as a petty, egoistic, insincere and dependent person, who has only ever striven to conceal the
weaknesses of his nature, he may as far as we know have
come quite close to self-knowledge, and we can only
wonder why one must become ill in order to have access
to such truth. For there can be no doubt that anyone
who has reached such an assessment of himself, and
expresses it to others – an assessment like that which
Prince Hamlet has ready for himself and everyone else
– is sick, whether he is telling the truth or treating himself
more or less unjustly. And it is not difficult to observe
that there is, in our judgement, no correspondence
between the extent of self-abasement and its justification
in reality. A hitherto well-behaved, efficient and dutiful
woman will not speak of herself more favourably in
melancholia than a woman who is really negligent of
her household; in fact the former is more likely to fall ill
with melancholia than the latter, a person about whom
we ourselves would be unable to find anything good to
say. Finally, we must be struck by the fact that the
melancholic does not behave just as someone contrite
with remorse and self-reproach would normally do. The
shame before others that characterizes the latter state
is missing, or at least not conspicuously present. In
the melancholic one might almost stress the opposite
trait of an insistent talkativeness, taking satisfaction from
self-exposure.

It is not, then, crucially important whether the melancholic is being accurate in his painful self-disparagement
when this criticism coincides with the judgement of

others. It is more a question of him providing an accurate description of his psychological situation. He has lost his self-esteem, and must have good reason for doing so. Then we find ourselves facing a contradiction which presents us with a mystery that is difficult to solve. Following the analogy with mourning, we were obliged to conclude that he has suffered a loss of object; his statements suggest a loss of his ego.

Before we address ourselves to this contradiction, let us linger for a while over the insight that the emotion of the melancholic gives us into the constitution of the human ego. In him, we see how one part of the ego presents itself to the other, critically assesses it and, so to speak, takes it as its object. Our suspicion that the critical agency which has split off from the ego in this case might also be able to demonstrate its autonomy under other circumstances is confirmed by all further observations. We will actually find a reason for separating this agency from the rest of the ego. What we are seeing here is the agency that is commonly called conscience; we will count it among the great institutions of the ego, along with censorship of consciousness and reality-testing, and somewhere we will find the proofs that it can become ill on its own account. The clinical picture of melancholia stresses moral disapproval of the patient's own ego over other manifestations: the subject will far more rarely judge himself in terms of physical affliction, ugliness, weakness and social inferiority; only impoverishment assumes a privileged position among the patient's anxieties or assertions.

One observation, and one that is not even difficult to

make, leads to an explanation of the contradiction set out above. If we listen patiently to the many and various self-reproaches of the melancholic, we will be unable to avoid a sense that the most intense among them often have little to do with the patient himself, but may with slight modifications be adapted to another person whom the patient loves, has loved or is supposed to love. Each time we look into the facts, the patient confirms this supposition. This means that we have in our hands the key to the clinical picture, recognizing self-reproaches as accusations against a love-object which have taken this route and transferred themselves to the patient's own ego.

The woman who loudly pities her husband for being bound to such a useless woman is actually seeking to accuse her husband of uselessness, in whatever sense the term may be used. We should not be too surprised that some authentic self-reproaches are scattered among those applied to the speaker; they may come to the fore because they help to conceal the others and to impede knowledge of the actual facts, since they emerge from the pros and cons of the conflict of love that has led to the loss of love. Now the behaviour of the patients also becomes much more comprehensible. Their laments [*Klagen*] are accusations [*Anklagen*], in the old sense of the German word; they are not ashamed, they do not conceal themselves, because everything disparaging that they express about themselves is basically being said about someone else; and they are a long way away from communicating to those around them the humility and submissiveness that would befit such unworthy people;

rather they are aggravating to a very high degree, they always seem as though they have been slighted, and as though a great wrong has been done to them. All of this is possible only because their reactions, as seen in their behaviour, still emanate from the mental constellation of rejection, which has, as the result of a certain process, been transferred to melancholic remorse.

There is then no difficulty in reconstructing this process. An object-choice had occurred, a bond had been formed between the libido and a particular person; through the influence of a real slight or disappointment on the part of the beloved person, that object-relation had been subjected to a shock. The result of this was not the normal one of the withdrawal of the libido from this object and its displacement on to a new one, but another, which seems to require a number of different conditions in order to come into being. Investment in objects proved not to be very resistant, and was suspended. The free libido was not, however, displaced on to another object, but instead drawn back into the ego. But it did not find any application there, serving instead to produce an identification of the ego with the abandoned object. In this way the shadow of the object fell upon the ego, which could now be condemned by a particular agency as an object, as the abandoned object. Thus the loss of object had been transformed into a loss of ego, and the conflict between the ego and the beloved person into a dichotomy between ego-criticism and the ego as modified by identification.

Some things may immediately be guessed about the preconditions and results of such a process. On the one hand a strong fixation on the love object must be present, but on the other hand, and in contradiction to that fixation, there must be minimal resistance in the form of object-investment. This contradiction seems to require the object-choice, in accordance with a telling observation by Otto Rank, to have occurred on a narcissistic foundation, so that the object-investment, if it encounters difficulties, is able to regress to narcissism. The narcissistic identification with the object then becomes the substitute for the love-investment, with the result that the love relationship, despite the conflict with the loved one, must not be abandoned. This substitution of identification for object-love is a significant mechanism for the narcissistic illnesses. K. Landauer recently uncovered it in the treatment of a case of schizophrenia. It naturally corresponds to the regression of a type of object-choice to original narcissism. Elsewhere we have explained that identification is the preliminary stage of object-choice, and the first way, ambivalent in its manifestation, in which the ego selects an object. It may assimilate this object, and, in accordance with the oral or cannibalistic phase of libido development, may do so by eating it. Abraham is probably right in tracing the rejection of nourishment, which is apparent in severe forms of the melancholic state, back to this connection.

The conclusion which the theory calls for, and which would transfer the predisposition to melancholic illness, or a part of it, to the predominance of the narcissistic type of object-choice, has unfortunately not been confirmed by investigation. In the introductory sentences of this paper I have confessed that the empirical material on which this study is based is inadequate for our claims. Were we able to assume an agreement between observation and our deductions, we should not hesitate in seeing the oral phase of the libido, which still belongs to narcissism, as one of the characteristics of melancholia. Identifications with the object are by no means rare, even in transference neuroses, and are indeed a well-known mechanism of symptom-formation, particularly in hysteria. But we may see the difference between narcissistic and hysterical identification as lying in the fact that in the former the object-investment is relinquished, while in the latter it continues to exist and manifests an effect that is usually restricted to certain individual actions and innervations. Even in the case of transference neuroses, identification is the manifestation of something held in common that may signify love. Narcissistic identification is the older of the two, and grants us access to an understanding of the less well-studied hysterical form.

So melancholia derives some of its characteristics from mourning, and the rest from the process of regression from the narcissistic object-choice to narcissism. On the one hand it is, like mourning, a reaction to the real loss of the love-object, but it also has a condition which either is absent from normal mourning or, where it is present, transforms it into pathological mourning. The loss of the love-object is an excellent opportunity for the ambivalence of love relationships to come to the fore. Consequently, where the predisposition to obsessive neurosis is present, the conflict of ambivalence gives mourning a pathological shape and forces it to manifest itself in the form of self-reproaches for having been oneself responsible for the loss of the love-object, of having wanted that loss. In such obsessive neurotic depressions after the death of loved ones we are shown what the conflict of ambivalence can achieve on its own when the regressive pull of the libido is not involved. For the most part, the causes of melancholia go beyond the clear case of loss through death, and include all the situations of insult, slight, setback and disappointment through which an opposition of love and hate can be introduced to the relationship, or an ambivalence already present can be intensified. This conflict of ambivalence, now more real, now more constitutive in origin, should not be neglected among the preconditions of melancholia. If the love of the object, which cannot be abandoned while the object itself is abandoned, has fled into narcissistic identification, hatred goes to work on this substitute object, insulting it, humiliating it, making it suffer and deriving a sadistic satisfaction from that suffering. The indubitably pleasurable self-torment of melancholia, like the corresponding phenomenon of obsessive neurosis, signifies the satisfaction of tendencies of sadism and hatred, which are applied to an object and are thus turned back against the patient's own person. In both of these illnesses, patients manage to avenge themselves on the original objects along the detour of self-punishment, and to torment their loved ones by means of being ill, having taken to illness in order to avoid showing their hostility directly. The person who provoked in the patient the emotional disturbance from which his form of illness took its orientation will generally be found in the patient's immediate milieu. Thus the melancholic's love-investment in his object has undergone a second fate; in part it has regressed to identification, but it has also been moved back, under the influence of the conflict of ambivalence, to the sadistic stage to which it is closer.

It is this sadism that solves the mystery of the inclination to suicide which makes melancholia both so interesting and so dangerous. We have acknowledged this great self-love of the ego as the primal state from which the life of the drives emanates, and we see in the anxiety that appears when our lives are endangered the liberation of so much narcissistic libido that we cannot grasp how the ego could ever consent to self-destruction. Certainly, we have known for a long time that no neurotic nurtures suicidal intentions who does not turn them back from an impulse to murder others, but we have achieved no understanding of the play of forces that could turn such an intention into action. Now the analysis of melancholia teaches us that the ego can only kill itself when it is able to treat itself as an object because of the return of object-investment, if it is able to direct the hostility that applies to the object back against itself and represents the original reaction of the ego against objects in the outside world. (See 'Drives and Their Fates'.) Thus in the regression of the narcissistic object-choice the object may have been abolished, but it has proved more potent than the ego itself. In the two contrasting situations of extreme passion and suicide the ego, although in entirely different ways, is overwhelmed by the object.

Hence, as regards the one particularly striking characteristic of melancholia, the emergence of the fear of impoverishment, it seems natural to trace it back to anal eroticism, torn from its context and regressively transformed.

Melancholia confronts us with other questions which to some extent it fails to answer. The fact that it passes after a certain amount of time, without leaving any broad or demonstrable changes, is a characteristic that it shares with mourning. It was there that we observed that time is required for the detailed implementation of the reality-testing command, after which the ego's libido is freed from the lost object. We may consider the ego busy with an analogous task during melancholia; in neither case do we have an economic understanding of its origin. The sleeplessness of melancholia testifies to the inflexibility of the condition, the impossibility of implementing the general drawing-in of investments required for sleep. The complex of melancholia behaves like an open wound, drawing investment energies to itself from all sides (energies which we have, in the case of transference neuroses, called 'counter-investments'), and draining the ego to the point of complete impoverishment; it can easily prove to be resistant to the ego's desire to sleep.

One element which is probably somatic, and which cannot be explained psychogenetically, becomes apparent in the regular alleviation of the condition that occurs in the evening. These considerations raise the question of whether the loss of the ego, regardless of the object (purely narcissistic injury to the ego) is enough to produce the image of melancholia, and whether an impoverishment of the ego-libido by the consumption of toxins can produce certain forms of the illness.

The most curious property of melancholia, and the one most in need of explanation, lies in its tendency to turn into the symptomatically opposite state of mania. As we know, this is not the fate of all cases of melancholia. Some cases develop in periodic relapses, the intervals between which reveal either no hint of mania at all, or only a very slight degree of it. Others demonstrate the regular alternation of melancholic and manic phases that has found expression in the formulation of cyclical insanity. One would be tempted to exclude these cases as being psychogenetic, had psychoanalytic treatment not brought about a therapeutic solution in several cases of this kind. So it is not only permissible, but actually imperative, to extend an analytic explanation of melancholia to mania as well.

I cannot promise that this attempt will be entirely satisfactory. In fact it does not go far beyond the possibility of an initial orientation. We have two clues at our disposal here, the first a psychoanalytical impression, the second what we might call a universal economic experience. The impression already expressed by a number of psychoanalytical researchers suggests that mania is not different in content from melancholia, that both illnesses battle with the same 'complex' to which the ego probably succumbs in melancholia, while in mania it has overcome it or pushed it aside. The other clue comes from the experience that in all states of joy, jubilation and triumph shown by the normal model of mania, the same economic conditions are apparent. As the result of a particular influence, a large expenditure of psychical energy, maintained over a long period or frequently recurring, finally becomes superfluous, and thus becomes available for many different applications and possibilities of discharge. Thus, for example: if a poor devil is suddenly relieved of his chronic concern about his daily bread by winning a large amount of money, if a long and strenuous struggle is finally crowned by success, if a person suddenly becomes capable of abandoning some pressing compulsion, a false position that he has had to maintain for a long time, and so on. All such situations are marked by a lightened mood, the signs of discharge of joyful emotion, and the intensified readiness for all kinds of actions, just like mania, and in complete contrast to the depression and inhibition of melancholia. One might dare to say that mania is in fact just such a triumph, except that what it has overcome, the source of its triumph, is hidden from the ego. Alcoholic intoxication, which belongs in the same series of states – albeit a more cheerful one – can be explained in much the same way; here there is probably a suggestion, accomplished by toxins, of the expenditure of repression. Lay opinion likes to assume that one is so keen on movement and activity in such a manic state because one is in 'such a cheerful mood'. Of course we will have to unmake this false connection. The economic state within the mental life which we mentioned above has been fulfilled, and that is why we are on the one hand so cheerful, and on the other so uninhibited in our actions.

If we combine these two suggestions, what we find is this: in mania, the ego must have overcome the loss of the object (or mourning over the loss, or perhaps the object itself), and now the total amount of counter-investment that the painful suffering of melancholia had drawn and bound to itself from the ego has become available. The manic person also unmistakably demonstrates his liberation from the object from which he had been suffering by pouncing on his new object-investments like a ravenous man.

This explanation may sound plausible, but first of all it is too vague, and secondly it throws up more new questions and doubts than we can answer. We do not wish to avoid discussing it, even though we cannot expect to find our way to clarity as a result.

In the first place, normal mourning also overcomes the loss of the object while at the same time absorbing all the energies of the ego during the period of its existence. Why, then, once it has run its course, is there not so much as a hint of the economic condition required for a phase of triumph? I cannot give a simple answer to this objection. It also draws our attention to the fact that we cannot even identify the economic means through which mourning accomplishes its task. However, a conjecture might come to our assistance here. To each individual memory and situation of expectation that shows the libido to be connected to the lost object, reality delivers its verdict that the object no longer exists, and the ego, presented with the question, so to speak, of whether it wishes to share this fate, is persuaded by the sum of narcissistic satisfactions that it derives from being alive to loosen its bonds with the object that has been destroyed. We might perhaps imagine that this process of dissolution takes place so slowly and gradually that by the time it is over the expenditure of energy required for its accomplishment has been dispersed.

It is tempting to try to proceed from conjecture about the work of mourning to an account of the work of melancholia. Here, at the outset, we encounter an uncertainty. Hitherto, we have hardly considered melancholia from the topographical point of view, and neither have we asked in and between which psychical systems the work of melancholia occurs. What part of the psychical processes of the disorder is still taking place in relation to the abandoned unconscious object-investments, and what part in relation to their substitute through identification, in the ego?

The quick and easy answer to this is that the 'unconscious (thing-)representation of the object by the libido is abandoned'. But in fact this representation consists of countless individual impressions (or their unconscious traces), and this withdrawal of the libido cannot be a matter of a moment, but must certainly, as in mourning, be a long drawn-out and gradual process. It is not easy to tell whether it begins simultaneously in many different places, or whether it contains some kind of sequence; in analytic treatment one can often observe that now this, now that memory is activated, and that the identical-sounding laments, tiresome in their monotony, have a different unconscious explanation each time. If the object does not have such a great significance for the ego, one that is intensified by thousands of connections, its loss is not apt to lead to mourning or melancholia. The characteristic of detaching the libido piecemeal can thus be attributed equally to melancholia and mourning; it is probably based on the same economic relations and serves the same tendencies in both.

But melancholia, as we have heard, contains more than normal mourning does. In melancholia, the relationship with the object is not a simple one, it is complicated by the conflict of ambivalence. That ambivalence is either constitutional, that is, it is attached to every love relationship of this particular ego, or else it emerges straight out of experiences that imply the threat of the loss of the object. In its causes, then, melancholia can go far beyond mourning, which is as a rule unleashed only by real loss, the death of the object. Thus in melancholia a series of individual battles for the object begins, in which love and hatred struggle with one another, one to free the libido from the object, the other to maintain the existing libido position against the onslaught. These individual battles cannot be transferred to a system other than the unconscious, the realm of memory traces of things (as against verbal investments). It is in this very place that attempts at solution are played out in mourning, but here they face no obstacle, since these processes continue on their normal way to consciousness through the preconscious. This path is closed to the work of melancholia, perhaps because of the large number of causes or because of the fact that they are all working together. Constitutional ambivalence essentially belongs to the repressed, and the traumatic experiences with the object may have activated other repressed material. Thus everything about these battles of ambivalence remains withdrawn from consciousness until the characteristic outcome of melancholia has been reached. As we know, this consists in the threatened libido-investment finally leaving the object, only to return to the place in the ego from which it had emerged. So it is by taking flight into the ego that love escapes abolition. After this regression of the libido, the process can become conscious, and represents itself to consciousness as a conflict between one part of the ego and the critical agency.

So what consciousness learns about in the work of melancholia is not the essential part of it, nor is it the part to which we may attribute an influence to the solution of suffering. We see the ego debasing itself and raging against itself, and have as little understanding as the patient about where that can lead and how it can change. We can more readily attribute such an accomplishment to the unconscious part of the work, because it is not difficult to discover a significant analogy between the work of melancholia and that of mourning. Just as mourning imples the ego to renounce the object by declaring its death, and offers the ego the reward of staying alive, each individual battle of ambivalence loosens the fixation of the libido upon the object by devaluing, disparaging and, so to speak, even killing it. There is a possibility of the process in the unconscious coming to an end, either once the fury has played itself out or after the object has been abandoned as worthless. We cannot tell which of these two possibilities brings melancholia to an end, either in all cases or in most, and what influence this termination has upon the further development of the case. The ego may enjoy the satisfaction of acknowledging itself to be the better of the two, and superior to the object.

Even if we accept this view of the work of melancholia, there is still one point upon which we were seeking enlightenment that it does not help to explain. We expected that an explanation of the economic condition for the emergence of mania with the passing of melancholia might be found in the ambivalence that dominates the disorder; this might find support in analogies drawn from various other areas. But there is one fact before which that expectation must bow. Of the three preconditions for melancholia: the loss of the object, ambivalence and the regression of the libido into the ego, we find the first two once more in the obsessive reproaches that we encounter after someone has died. There, it is beyond a doubt ambivalence that represents the main driving force of the conflict, and observation shows that once it has passed, nothing of the triumph of a manic constitution remains. This leads us to the third element as the sole factor responsible. The accumulation of investment, which is freed once the work of melancholia is concluded, and which makes mania possible, must be linked to the regression of the libido to narcissism. The conflict within the ego which melancholia exchanges for the battle over the object must behave like a painful wound requiring an extraordinarily high counter-investment. But here, once again, it makes sense for us to come to a halt and put off any further explanation of mania until we have gained an insight into the economic nature first of physical pain and then of the mental pain analogous to it. We know already that the interdependence of the complex problems of the psyche requires us to break off each investigation before it is completed – until the results of some other investigation can come to its aid.

(1917)

THE STORY OF PENGUIN CLASSICS

Before 1946 ... 'Classics' are mainly the domain of academics and students; readable editions for everyone else are almost unheard of. This all changes when a little-known classicist, E. V. Rieu, presents Penguin founder Allen Lane with the translation of Homer's *Odyssey* that he has been working on in his spare time.

1946 Penguin Classics debuts with *The Odyssey*, which promptly sells three million copies. Suddenly, classics are no longer for the privileged few.

1950s Rieu, now series editor, turns to professional writers for the best modern, readable translations, including Dorothy L. Sayers's *Inferno* and Robert Graves's unexpurgated *Twelve Caesars*.

1960s The Classics are given the distinctive black covers that have remained a constant throughout the life of the series. Rieu retires in 1964, hailing the Penguin Classics list as 'the greatest educative force of the twentieth century.'

1970s A new generation of translators swells the Penguin Classics ranks, introducing readers of English to classics of world literature from more than twenty languages. The list grows to encompass more history, philosophy, science, religion and politics.

1980s The Penguin American Library launches with titles such as *Uncle Tom's Cabin*, and joins forces with Penguin Classics to provide the most comprehensive library of world literature available from any paperback publisher.

1990s The launch of Penguin Audiobooks brings the classics to a listening audience for the first time, and in 1999 the worldwide launch of the Penguin Classics website extends their reach to the global online community.

The 21st Century Penguin Classics are completely redesigned for the first time in nearly twenty years. This world-famous series now consists of more than 1300 titles, making the widest range of the best books ever written available to millions – and constantly redefining what makes a 'classic'.

The Odyssey continues ...

The best books ever written

PENGUIN ⦿ CLASSICS

SINCE 1946

Find out more at www.penguinclassics.com